EGENDS

BIG GAME FISHING

THE MEN AND THEIR STORIES

EDITED AND COMPILED

BY

PATRICK MANSELL

Living Legends
of
Big Game Fishing

The Men and Their Stories

Edited and Compiled
by
Patrick Mansell

For information contact:
Bimini Twist Adventures, Inc.
2911 NW 27th Ave.
Boca Raton, FL 33434
(561) 451-3452

ISBN 0-9728564-7-1

Illustrations by Kevin Nakamaru - Kona, HI
Design by Paul Hammond-Studio 41- Boca Raton, FL

Manufactured in the United States of America

Though this be madness,
there is method in it.
William Shakespeare

TABLE OF CONTENTS

Acknowledgments   i

Forward   v

Preface   i x

Ron Hamlin   3
    Fire Onboard the Premier Cru   6
    Captain Without a Clue   11
    Guatemala Big Game Fishing   17

Bart Miller   23
    The Story of 1656   28
    TuTu   37
    Tuna Samurai   43

Peter Bristow   58
    Only One Fish   62

Brazakka   83
    Lee's Last Fish (Lee Marvin)   91
    A Grand Tale   96

Bobby Brown   105
    The Underwater Wiremens' Club   113
    Mike's Second Trip Overboard   118
    The Day I Joined the Club   121
    Double Doubles at Kalea   124

Kevin Nakamaru   132
   My First Season in Madeira   136

Peter Wright   148
   A Marlin to Remember   151

Bouncer Smith   160
   My Greatest Fishing Adventure   163
   Tarpon   167
   Jerks Can't Use Circle Hooks   174

Skip Smith   179
   So Many Firsts/ Swordfish off South Africa   181

Bark Garnsey   194
   Nickie Campbell's Madeira Adventure   197

Billy Harrison   207
   Blue Fins off Bimini   210

George Poveromo   228
   Madness at the Buoy   230
   Dolphin on the Troll   236

ACKNOWLEDGMENTS

It took a lot of people to help put this book together. I could have never done this without their cooperation and generous assistance. The project started out as an idea that was probably too big to take on alone. I contacted a few of these legendary captains to see if they thought the idea of telling of their vast experiences and letting us in on some of the secrets of their techniques would be of interest to anyone. No one had ever done something like this with men of such stature in the sportfishing world. Early to jump on board were Captains Bouncer Smith and Ron Hamlin. With their agreement to be a part of the project I had a running start.

At a book signing several years ago at the prestigious Miami Beach Rod and Reel Club, I met one of the top names in marlin fishing today. At the time I was promoting my first two books, *Bimini Twist* and *Abaco Gold*, and Peter Wright walked up and looked over my books. I knew who the guy was, everyone knows who he is. He's the preeminent marlin fisherman on the scene today and a recognized leader in marine conservation. I gave him a copy of one of my books and signed it for his daughter. So that was when I got to meet Peter Wright. Now, several years later, I figured I had nothing to lose by trying to bring him on board. I found his email address and sent a note describing the book project and asking if he'd join the group. Not only did he say yes, first cautioning me that he had a hectic schedule and he would see what he could do, he also told me that if I was going to do this project, I ought to contact Bart Miller, Peter Bristow and Brazakka.

The way I followed up was by contacting these men, telling them right off the bat that Peter Wright told me to contact them, and described the project to them. Very fortunately all three answered in the affirmative.

Since that time over a year ago I have met with Bart Miller on several occasions and try to speak with him at least a few times a month. Bart has helped me every step of the way. Many of these men he knows personally, and several of them are very close friends of his. He has guided my hand in the production of this book, keeping doors open for me, advising me, introducing me to a few of the fellows and taking me to task when I've done things other than how he wanted me to do them. Bart is a challenge because in his own right he is an excellent writer in addition to his vast accomplishments as a big game captain. We did not agree on every aspect of the book, but I think we're good enough friends that we can overlook our differences and continue our intellectual and philosophical banter for a long time to come.

In mid-February of '05, the Miami International Boat Show created several opportunities for me. One was that Peter Bristow was coming to town all the way from Madeira to meet up with some friends and do some business. Knowing he was coming, we made arrangements to meet up while he was here for the show. We spent parts of three days together and the time was very productive for this book. We did some work on his story about JoJo Del Guercio and spent many hours talking about a proper framework for this book. At that time he introduced me to Billy Harrison who is a world class giant blue fin tuna fisherman and an accomplished photographer as well. Billy has been exceedingly generous with his time in not only contributing his story for the book, but has also visited me several times and we have spoken dozens of times on the phone not only about his work, but also about the work of many others. He knows the Who's Who of big game fishing and his lifetime of fishing adventures on nearly every continent could fill several volumes on their own.

Also unknown to me until the boat show was one of the really important contributors to this book, Kevin Nakamaru. I was visiting Bart Miller at his company's booth where he displays the the highest quality custom fishing gear on the planet under the trademark of Black Bart Lures. Bart gestured over toward Kevin who was standing only about twenty feet away. He told me that this man represents the new generation of big game fishing legends. In addition to being an acknowledged fishing great, Kevin is also an accomplished marine artist. I had a heck of a time getting Kevin to agree to write for my book. In his modesty he did not believe he should be counted among the greats like Bart Miller, Peter Wright, Peter Bristow, Ron Hamlin or Bobby Brown. But greatness is more subjective than objective, so I cajoled him to join up. And not only did he agree to tell his story, but he also agreed to provide artwork to go along with the stories. The sketches within these pages were provided by Kevin and drawn exclusively for this book. For this I am eternally grateful to Kevin. He helped turn a work of literature into a work of art.

When dealing with people on the complete opposite side of the world, there's practically no time when a phone call is convenient. I very much wanted the famous outdoorsman from Down Under, Brazakka, to be a part of this work. With our busy schedules and opposite time zones we were not having an easy time of it trying to connect. The solution came in the form of Brazakka's closest friend, Paul Kidd. Paul is an avid sports enthusiast himself, and a professional writer. Without his early intervention and unwavering support there would be no Brazakka stories and this book would be so much less without it.

The two Merritt boats on the cover are taken from a photograph contributed by Coco Pale ologos. My sincerest thanks goes out to Coco for his generosity in allowing us to use this image.

There are two other people who are a part of all my books and who worked hard on this one as well. First, my wife Lisa offered constant encouragement while I spent a year and a half putting the book together. She also assisted with the proof reading. It's a thankless job but a necessary one, and one for which I am ever grateful. And second is my good friend Paul Hammond who did most of the design work and cover graphics for the book. Paul has an awesome talent for creating cover art that makes people give my books a second, third and fourth look.

And thanks to all of the participants who took the time to write their stories, sit through numerous personal interviews, and respond to dozens of e-mails. While I have been given the privilege of meeting and working with these Living Legends of Big Game Fishing, it is only they who have made this book possible.

FORWARD

Peter Bristow sat in my Fort Lauderdale office and was passionate about making a single point. In creating the Living Legends project, I needed to understand an important point: The last fifty years of innovation in big-game fishing have seen a revolution in the industry. The new equipment and techniques being used today are a result of research, both on and off the water, by industry professionals. And much of that innovation has come out of the great masters of fishing who are, or have been, connected to the South Florida fishing scene. That put me in the perfect place to network with some of the greatest fishermen in the world to compile this book.

So what do each of these men have in common that have taught them how to find and attract fish where mere mortals fail? How about thirty or forty years on the bridge or in the tower, trolling baits and lures, in every corner of the world. These men are all as different as night and day, but they all possess certain traits that make them similar. First and foremost, of course, is their love of fishing. In that respect I have not, in a single instance of dealing with them, found a great fisherman who was indifferent. In fact, what I have found is enthusiasm that never turns off.

In reading the biographies of these men, it appears that most got their start as professional fishermen in a very humble place, most on the various charter docks around the Atlantic and Pacific oceans. Some were mates, some sold bait, some had commercial fishing backgrounds. We might be inclined to assign such trades with minimal skill or education levels, kind of a blue collar mind set. But we would be so wrong to categorize them thus. My experience of these men has been that every one of them is very intelligent, quite articulate, and very creative. In fact the cloth these men were cut from would have allowed them to be successful at whatever profession or trade they chose. It's just that they are passionate about fishing and have directed their efforts that way. Because of their focus and dedication they have led interesting lives, have mingled with every kind of humanity from the lowliest bottom scraper to the highest celebrity, industrialist or politician. And, at the end of the day, they have had experiences that most of us can only imagine.

Anyone who has ever spent a day on the water knows that all kinds of adventures can come your way. It might be some crazy weather, a wild wave, an amazing fish, turtle or bird. It can be a serious mishap that threatens or takes a life. The ocean can be a fun playground, but it can also be a very dangerous place. Bart Miller expressed it beautifully when he wrote, "The sea has many faces, not all of them peaceful, playful, or fun." And as Ron Hamlin put it in his story *Fire Onboard the Premier Cru*, "Bad things can happen fast!" And of course, good things can happen fast too.

And that's where this book comes in. These exciting, intriguing, exceptional Living Legends of Big Game Fishing have stories to tell. They have seen it all. In fact each of them could write his own book about the wonderful, amazing, spectacular and tragic events he has experienced and witnessed.

When putting this project together I asked each of them to tell a story that had significance to them. Tell of an adventure, a spectacular fish, a technique or opinion they would like to share. They were given a blank page on which they were asked to talk about something that was exciting, or different, a life changing experience, or just whatever it was that they thought might interest others. And did they ever come up with the goods! At times I would read their articles or listen to their tapes and my jaw would drop. Sometimes it seemed inconceivable that people had the strength to live through some of the things these men have experienced. How crazy is it to land a bluefin tuna that weighs in excess of 900 pounds? I still haven't been in the cockpit of a boat that was hooked to a thousand pound blue or black marlin. Most of these guys have made that happen many times. To them it's all in a day's work. To the average person it's a life altering experience.

While working on this project I have been asked many times about the men themselves. I guess that people assume that men who reach this level in any profession are full of themselves, egomaniacs, Type A competitors. Anyhow, that's what I was asked. How difficult were they? How crusty are they? What's it like to be around men who reach such a high plateau in such a rugged profession? To be honest, I always knew that each of them belonged on this A list of fishing greats. Quite a few of them were humble enough to believe they had no business in this company. They were anything but egotistical or difficult. I found them mostly to be, first of all, passionate about fishing, then intelligent, curious and creative. Most had plenty of salt under their fingernails, but I found none of them to be conceited, arrogant or difficult. They were eager to talk about their sport and anxious to share their experiences. I might have had some difficulty rounding everyone up to get their stories in, but remember, these are very busy men, booked solid for months ahead and traveling all over the world. Moving targets, so to speak.

And what about rivalries between these captains and each other, and with other captains who are not a part of this project? My observation has been that any rivalry that I have noted probably falls within the 'healthy' range. When you look at the records of men like Peter Wright, Bart Miller, Bobby Brown, Ron Hamlin or Peter Bristow, and I could add all of our captains to this list, who do they really need to impress? They've been so successful at big-game, deep-sea fishing that their records speak for themselves. It would be beneath them to get too caught up in bragging rights and one-upmanship. I have witnessed very little of that kind of behavior while assembling these stories.

So, I invite you to strap yourself in and get ready for a different kind of ride. This one is way offshore in very deep and blue water. Take comfort in the knowledge that you can relax in your favorite easy chair and enjoy these experiences with the Living Legends of Big Game Fishing while they do all the heavy lifting.

PREFACE

A number of famous captains and anglers expressed an interest in contributing articles to the Living Legends book. And some of them had the stature to include their names among those who were finally selected. But, at the end of the day, I had to ask myself how have these participants evolved after their so many decades of fishing for the world's great game fish? What I believe separates these living legends from many other famous captains and anglers is their transformation from being users of the ocean's resources to being protectors of the ocean's resources. Each of these men has seen his share of waste at the weigh station as captains and anglers strive for a new world record or a tournament title. And each has come to the realization that what was fashionable in the 1960's, 70's and 80's, was not going to be acceptable in the 1990's, and certainly not in the twenty-first century. No longer do fishing enthusiasts laud the captain who hangs the carcass of a Pacific sail or inedible tarpon on a hook for spectators to gawk at in hopes of snaring a charter for a future day. Anyone who fishes for fun and sport and cares about the future of our fisheries knows well enough to throw back the undersized catches and keep only what he can use. The ocean's resources are limited and they are stressed out.

The men who made it into this book know this and live by it. There are no regrets for the way they fished decades ago as that was how it was done. But now the measure of the man and how he will be judged by his peers will depend more upon what he sets free than what he takes. Hanging the carcasses of rare, exotic or endangered fish is just not politically correct anymore. In fact it is unforgivable and grotesque. Sports fishermen, if they are to be called sports, know this lesson and pass it on to others.

This book carries a few pictures of dead fish because they are an important part of the history of big game fishing. Most are records of inestimable importance in the sport. And because they have been shown for the magnificent animals they are or were, a greater appreciation can be had by all for knowing them better.

I have a very good feeling about the direction sport fishing is going when it comes to conservation. It's coming around to where the guy who takes a twelve gauge pump and massacres a 350 pound hammerhead shark so he can hang it at the dock and draw a crowd, is going to be shunned. The guy who tags a healthy blue marlin and releases it so it can go on to make babies and live another twenty years is the hero.

To a man, every contributor to this book knows, understands and preaches conservation. I have conducted hundreds of interviews in the making of the book and never has one of these captains boasted about the fish they killed. They are the leaders in the sport and have lived through the transformation in attitudes, and now stand out as the respected voices on the subject of ocean conservation. I have been motivated by these men to help them to tell these stories because in the end the oceans can only be saved through awareness of their condition.

It was a heartwarming experience to be present at the Annual Awards Presentation of The Billfish Foundation at the Miami Beach Rod and Reel Club in February 2005. I consider The Billfish Foundation an important resource in the awareness and preservation of pelagic species. Here there are no honors for line class world record catches. Only T&R (tag and release) is respected. This is where important research is being conducted into the spawning habits and migration patterns of all kinds of billfish. At this gathering many of the top ocean scientists and fishing enthusiasts in the world come together to honor their own. It was awesome to see the entire room stand and give an ovation to Ron Hamlin, known to insiders as Captain Hook, as their "Man of the Year". Ron has released over 20,000 billfish in his career and has been the foremost voice in favor of circle hooks since the things were invented. I believe that after his so many years on the bridge and his decades of educating fishermen through his example and emails, Ron stands out as perhaps the most important captain of them all. It is for this reason that he is the lead-off storyteller in this book.

So, as you read these stories and view the pictures, don't be judgmental if some of the scenes and tales are in shades that do not perfectly please your sensibilities. That was then and this is now, and we had to go there to get where we are today.

Captain
Ron Hamlin

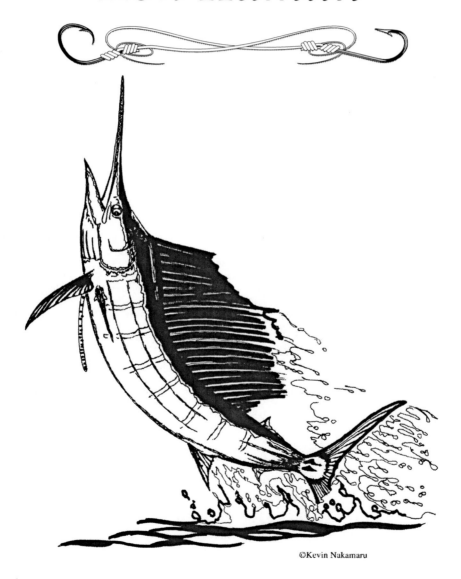

©Kevin Nakamaru

CAPTAIN RON HAMLIN

Ron Hamlin began his professional fishing career in 1959 in Boynton Beach, Florida on board the charter boat *Lucky Penny*. From there he began chartering out of Palm Beach with Capt. Frank Ardine where he was first introduced to tagging. In 1967 Ron got his first job as a captain. Later, in the early 1970's, Ron ran the *Big Blue* for Jerry Bos, and in 1971 Jerry took Ron to Australia where he caught his first grander, a 1,098 pound black marlin on board *Kalimar*.

Ron then took the captain's job on Joe Lopez's boat, *Prowess*, shuffling throughout the Atlantic and Caribbean. During this time he developed the process for formaldehyde mackerel. This invention allowed anglers to fast-troll for marlin using dead baits, and in 1974 and 1975 they caught more blue marlins than any other boat in the Atlantic Ocean. It was sailfish in Cozumel, marlin in St. Thomas and giant tuna in Cat Cay. In 1975 *Prowess* was the first American boat to discover the excellent fishing off Venezuela and had a great deal of success with sails, blues, swords and, of course, white marlin. In 1977 Ron took time off from fishing to write the Doubleday book *Tournament*. Soon thereafter he returned to fishing throughout the Atlantic and Carribean. During this time between the 1980's until 1994 he caught upwards of about 3,000 billfish.

Then in 1994, at the strong urging of his friend Tim Choate, Ron moved to Guatemala where the sail fishing is unequaled anywhere in the world. Bill Gooch bought the beautiful Carolina built forty-two foot Willis and named it *Captain Hook* after Ron's nickname of thirty years. Ron took over as captain and made this one of the most famous billfishing boats in the world. In Guatemala Ron became a serious enthusiast of tagging and pioneered the use of circle hooks with billfish. In the time since his arrival there, Ron has released 20,000 billfish, mostly sails, and has tagged more than 7,000 of them.

With over 40 years of experience on the bridge, Capt. Hamlin has earned a world class reputation as an award-winning sportfishing guide. He is also accomplished at offshore fly techniques and has held six world fly fishing records, four for sails, and one each for white and blue marlins. For his efforts at conservation of the billfish species with circle hooks and tagging and releasing, he has won many awards, but the one of which he is most proud is the NOAA Environmental Hero Award.

In addition to numerous tournament victories Capt. Hamlin has continued with a consistent pattern of awards and world records dating as far back as 1974 when he took his first world record for a fifty-six pound sailfish on twelve pound tippet. In 1977 he was also the first person to ever catch a swordfish in the Bahamas on rod and reel. In 1984 he established the records for the largest blue marlins ever caught in Venezuela and Puerto Rico, 1,023 and 984 pounds respectively. In that same year Capt. Hamlin set the world record for white marlin on fly. Other records and awards include the following:

1990- World record blue marlin on sixteen pound tippet

1997- award from the Billfish Foundation for most sailfish released, and Sportsman of the Year Award from Youth Club of South Florida for conservation work with circle hooks

1998- AFTCO Award for most sailfish released; most Pacific sailfish released in one day (71); since broken by himself; AFTCO Award for most sails tagged in the Pacific; AFTCO Captain of the Year

1999- World record sailfish on fly; AFTCO Award for most billfish tagged in one year (1600+); most billfish in one year (2,555); most sailfish on fly in one year (432)

2000- World record sailfish on 8 pound tippet; The Billfish Foundation's Top Release Captain; AFTCO award for Top Captain in the tagging category; Environmental Hero Award from NOAA for protection of the environment

2001- AFTCO Top Tagging Captain

The Billfish Foundation Top Sailfish Tagging Captain in the Pacific; The Billfish Foundation Captain of the Year *2002, 2003, 2004*

In 2005 on board *Captain Hook*, Ron's anglers tied *Pelagian's* world record of 27 sails caught on fly in a single day.

Capt. Hamlin's plans for the future include continuing his conservation efforts on behalf of the ocean's billfish and starting a school for young anglers to teach them the lessons he has learned over forty-five years of sport fishing.

FIRE ONBOARD THE PREMIER CRU
by
RON HAMLIN

I was bringing the forty-one foot Striker called *Premier Cru* up from St. Thomas. The year was 1982, and on board with me were two mates, Greg and Bait, and my fiancé, Danielle. We were at the end of a 400 mile leg to South Caicos, only thirteen miles left to go, and from the bridge, the Riding Rock Inn could be seen on the horizon. The Striker performed best at slower speeds and we were cruising at ten knots on the way in. At about 3:30 in the afternoon I decided that if I boosted the throttle a little, we would be able to make it in to port before Customs closed, thus avoiding the overtime we would otherwise have to pay if we arrived too late. I throttled up to about fourteen or fifteen knots, not the best performance speed for this boat, but with the island in view we could be in within the hour.

Meanwhile down in the engine room, what I believe was a faulty oil line ready to let go, must have had more stress than it could handle. The boat backed off its speed all by itself without my touching the throttles. This was not good. The hatch on the engine compartment was very tight so I could not hear anything that sounded wrong. I would just have to climb down off the bridge to see what was the matter.

The engine hatch was just inside the cabin. The instant I opened the cover to the compartment all hell broke loose. I believe that the fire had already started and was contained somewhat on account of the automatic CO2 system. It's possible that the CO2 had been keeping the fire under control, but it had not put it out completely. And because the oxygen in the compartment had been burned up, the fire did not have all the ingredients it needed to grow or spread. When I opened the engine hatch it set up a classical backdraft situation. Oxygen rushed into the compartment and fire leapt out and reached all the way to the cabin overhead. I reacted as quickly as I could, barely getting out of the way fast enough to avoid being burned. The instant the flames shot out of there, the fire was out of control. Our main fire control device had been used up and there was no time to stand there and throw water on it. I had a greater fear that something would soon explode and injure or kill one or all of us, so I made a quick decision to abandon everyone safely from the boat.

I yelled for everyone to head for the bow. I repeated this several times. Danielle and the mates had to climb through the cabin windows to get up to the bow. I was fortunate in that my briefcase that contained our money and passports was right at the side of the cabin doorway and I was able to grab it as I backed away. While Danielle and Greg and Bait were scrambling to get out onto the bow, I hustled up to the bridge. I knew the flames were right under me so I only had a few seconds to act. Knowing that the Riding Rock Inn monitored channel sixteen, I put out a Mayday on the radio.

Premier Cru had no life boat, but by some stroke of good luck while we were in St. Thomas we had found a small Zodiac about nine feet long. We used it as a utility boat for rowing around and snorkeling. When we headed to Caicos we hauled it up onto our bow and let it ride up there. In it at the time of the fire were a mask, fins and a half jug of water. While I was on the bridge calling in the Mayday and putting the engines into reverse with the auto pilot still on, Greg and Bait launched the Zodiac. Danielle grabbed a life preserver and all three of them jumped overboard and climbed into the Zodiac. I followed a few seconds behind them.

Within a minute or two, one of the engines shut down which caused the boat to move in circles. I was concerned that we might be in its erratic path, but that ended up not being a problem. From a distance we watched the boat become engulfed in flames. It was a burning, melting, stinking mass of diesel fuel from the tanks, aluminum from the hull, and a combination of those materials that were contained in the interior of the boat, including the furnishings, electronics, our clothes and all of our fishing gear and provisions. It was an impressive flame that I will never forget. Soon the stern started taking on water and it took only a few minutes for the boat to begin to sink. For awhile the one engine continued to run and then it too shut down. We watched as *Premier Cru* did its final death dance. Fire hissed and crackled as the hull sank deeper and deeper from the stern. And then as if in its final death throes, it sank beneath the surface and did not stop until it rested on the bottom.

From the bridge I had been able to see South Caicos Island. My eye level was about fifteen feet above the surface of the ocean. But from the Zodiac we were at sea level and could only see the horizon. While I knew which direction we needed to head to get to the island, Danielle was not so certain of that. She was terribly shook up from the experience, as we all were, and she was scared, as she had a right to be. I knew the direction we had to follow, because I knew the direction of the wind and currents. I knew they were favorable and in time we would end up pretty close to where we wanted to be. But Danielle questioned that and could not relax even for a minute.

We drifted for hours, through the evening and into the deep hours of the night. The moon came up, and undisturbed by any outside light source, our night vision was very good. Eventually we were able to make out a lump in the water that we guessed to be a small island. No matter what other options were or were not available to us, this island held much better possibilities for us than the Zodiac did. We used the fins as paddles and made our way up to the small coral outcropping. We could hear waves breaking against its shore so we knew we had to get around the other side of it in order to come ashore. A few more minutes of paddling and we were there. The coral rock was as sharp as glass and we had to be very careful climbing out of the boat. Once we were on shore we could not move around very much because we only had two pairs of shoes between us, and we had to hand them back and forth in order to move around. But in spite of everything, we knew we were on solid ground which greatly improved our chances of survival.

We had been soaked by the sea and cramped up in that small Zodiac for many hours. In the night the temperature had dropped precipitously and Danielle was most certainly suffering from hypothermia. As awful and jagged as the surface of the coral rock was, we had to lie down and try to give each other body warmth just to make it through the night. Danielle's condition was bad and I did not want it to worsen. We curled up together in a small ravine that offered only the slightest relief from the jagged rocks, but on account of our extreme exhaustion we were able to sleep.

I was awakened by Greg and Bait's yelling at a passing Bahamian lobster boat. We hailed the native lobster man over and told him of our dilemma of having lost our boat and struggling to get onto this small rock outcropping. The man said he had seen the smoke and fire of *Premier Cru* the day before, but he could not get out to us because of the sun setting in his eyes. Rescue was at hand and I did not want to jeopardize that, but at the same time I knew the man was lying. Our boat sank to the east of Caicos and the sun would have been setting behind the man. Anyhow, I didn't say anything about that. I just wanted to get my crew back to land. I asked the Bahamian to help us out. He balked because he had lobster to catch and he would lose money if he stopped now to help us. My urge was to put this man on the coral rock and take my crew back to Caicos in his boat. But I didn't want a hassle so I offered to double what the man would make this day by lobstering if he would give us a ride back in. He agreed. The lobster boat could not come ashore for fear of damage to the hull on the sharp rocks. No problem, we would jump in the water and swim over to him. But there was a problem I did not know about. Danielle had never told me that she could not swim. While I wanted to tear into her for being so stupid as to take an ocean voyage in a small boat without having this basic skill, this was not the time. I gently coaxed her into jumping into the water with the life preserver on and together we swam over to the boat.

It took a while to get settled once we reached land. There was Customs to clear and reports to make about the boat. We had to find a place to clean up and something to eat. The report of the sinking was made to the authorities and was made available to the boat's owner, Bill Reed, so he could file his insurance claim. When I spoke to Bill and told him of the loss of his boat, his only concern was for me and Danielle and the crew. He didn't even ask about the boat, he just wanted to be certain that we were all right. His concerns were in the right place for a good boat owner, and I have always appreciated that.

The Mayday I sent out was never received. The Riding Rock Inn was closed, so I'm not sure anyone anywhere ever heard my call. But I learned an important lesson that day. Even though I had at that time been a Captain for many years, there was a lesson here that everyone should learn. When there is a fire on board a vessel, there is very little time to react. Events happen in an instant and things go down hill at breakneck speed. Flames can engulf a boat in seconds, explosions can occur, even on diesel machines. Near panic sets in and split second decisions can mean the difference between a successful evacuation and rescue, and tragedy. It is always best to have a fire plan in place before the boat leaves the dock.

CAPTAIN WITHOUT A CLUE
by
RON HAMLIN

I was nineteen years old in the summer of 1963 when I ventured up to Atlantic City, New Jersey, to see what the action might be like and look for a job as a mate on one of the local charter boats. Upon arriving there I found that there were no jobs available for mates, but there was a job available for a captain. I told the owner that I was more of a mate than a captain, but he asked me if I knew how to run a boat. I said sure I could, and so he said I was hired. Naturally I was nervous about this responsibility but I had some friends up there who said they would help me out, keep me from getting lost and, in general, look out for me.

We were entered in the Atlantic City Tuna Tournament. For this tournament the committee would blow a clacton at five in the morning for the start of fishing. Since I was following two other boats that knew the way out, I could not be a minute late for the start. I told this to the the owner and his family and they agreed. My instructions to them were that we were to meet between 4:30 and 4:45, and no later.

The owner complied with my instructions and they were at the dock at exactly 4:45 AM. There was no time to waste, we had to just climb on board this thirty-seven foot wooden Peterson Viking named *What's Wrong*, and get ready for the starter's signal. In the party was the owner, his wife and son, and the son's fiancé. A nice family group that promised to be a couple of good days of fishing together. At quarter to five the son came to me and said he wanted to go eat breakfast. I told him that it was now too late as we had to be ready when the bell goes off because I was following two other boats out. We were heading out off Ocean City, Maryland to a place called the Jack Spot where we were going to fish. I didn't know a thing about being a captain or navigating or anything else, so I would have to follow my friends out. My thinking was that if they had enough fuel to get out there, then I must too.

We ran out to the southeast for about three hours. It was now about 8:00 AM when one of my engines quit. Knowing nothing about marine mechanics I went down and opened the engine hatch and looked around. I tapped on the carburetor, checked the spark plug wires and twisted the distributor cap, and then I was out of ideas of how to fix this problem. I closed the engine hatch and decided we'd have to continue on one engine. I got on the radio and told my friends that I wouldn't be able to follow them any longer. They said not to worry because there were 200 other boats in the tournament and there would be plenty of boats to follow in when we were done fishing. This was OK with me so I kept running.

About an hour later I spied some tuna jumping so I slowed the boat down and came down off the bridge to set up the cockpit. I didn't have a mate so I had to do everything myself. After a bit of a struggle I had four lines out and we were fishing. I ran back up to the bridge and began to circle around on the school when I heard the fiancé scream. I looked down to see the boy leaning over one of the rods in the transom and going into convulsions. He had fallen out of the chair, onto the rods and then onto the floor. He was going into uncontrollable spasms. He was kicking and shaking back and forth, side-to-side and was totally out of control. I came down from the bridge to try to get him under control. As I held on to him he shook me around as if I wasn't even there. Finally I put my feet up against the stanchion of the fighting chair and pinned him against the bulkhead. He could not squirm so much even though his head was still rolling and snapping from side-to-side.

The father began screaming, "Get a doctor, get a doctor!" The girlfriend was hysterical and the mother fainted dead away. I ran back up to the bridge and got on the radio. With 200 boats nearby, there had to be a doctor.

I called out on the radio. "This is the boat *What's Wrong*. We need a doctor. Is there a doctor out there?"

Right away a call came back to me from a doctor who had been monitoring his radio. "What's wrong? *What's Wrong*," came the reply.

I told him that this kid is going crazy down here, that he had fallen out of the chair and was jumping and shaking all around. I had him in a blanket and his feet elevated. This was just about the extent of my first aid knowledge. I didn't know anything else to do. Then the father called up to me that the boy was diabetic. I relayed this back to the doctor that the boy was diabetic. The doctor asked me if he had his insulin this morning. I asked the father if he'd had his insulin this morning. The father said yes, that he had given it to him. I said to the doctor, yes, the father gave it to him. Then the doctor asked has he had anything to eat this morning. I began calling down to the father to ask him had he eaten anything. Then I remembered that I had stopped him from going to breakfast over four hours earlier. I replied to the doctor that he had not eaten anything. The doctor immediately diagnosed the boy's problem as "sugar shock", what we know as an insulin reaction. He said if the boy were going to live he would have to be air-lifted to a hospital. He gave me instructions to try to get some sugar into him and that would help bring him out of this condition and might save his life.

I was told to put out a Mayday to the Coast Guard to have them bring a doctor out in a helicopter and treat him, and then bring the boy back in with them. I placed the call to the Coast Guard and tried as best I could to tell them my position. I had no GPS and I was far out of sight of land so all I could tell them is that I had run so many miles for such a length of time and let them figure out where I was. They instructed me to stay on the radio and they would triangulate off my radio signal. They soon located my position and dispatched two helicopters to find me and rescue the boy. By now I had attracted several other boats to my position who were curious and wanted to watch this fiasco.

As an immediate remedy to the boy's situation I was instructed to try and force some sugar into his mouth to combat the insulin reaction. We had some packets of sugar in the galley and so I got a few of them and proceeded to try to pour it into his mouth, but with his rolling of his head back and forth it was hard to get it to go into his mouth. There was a mountain of sugar surrounding his lips and on the edge of his mouth, but I had to somehow get it to go into his mouth. I found a pencil and used the eraser end to push the sugar over his lips and into his mouth. As I was pushing the eraser into the boy's mouth, imagine me kneeling over the boy and stuffing the eraser end of a pencil down his mouth, when his mother woke up. She looked over, saw what I was doing, and fainted all over again.

I asked the Coast Guard on the radio if there was anything he wanted me to do with the boat as he hovered above us. He said to do nothing. But as he hovered above me, the downdraft from the copter blades caused the boat to spin around. Soon they were lowering a doctor down from the helicopter onto the spinning deck of my little boat. As the boat kept moving away from the descending doctor, I got out the long handled gaff and caught him by the pants leg and started guiding him in. The doctor's feet finally touched down on the deck of the boat. He took off the horse collar that had been used to lower him from the helicopter, and the first thing he said was that he thought he was going to be sick. He had not been on the boat long enough to be seasick, he was actually sick from the helicopter ride out. For the first ten minutes onboard he puked over the side and moaned about his condition. When he felt just a little better he looked the boy over and gave him a shot and said that he would have to go to the hospital. We called the helicopter back over and told them that we were going to have to airlift the boy back to a hospital.

The helicopter came back and lowered a horse collar for us to put on the boy. We got the collar onto the boy and were now ready to hoist the boy up. I was standing on the covering board with one foot on the transom and the other on the side trying to help haul him up. The helicopter began lifting and I held on to steer him. Finally when I could feel the pressure of him being lifted, I let go of the boy, pushing him off so he would be free of the boat. But instead of him being lifted straight up, he was actually dropped back down into the water completely out of sight under the surface. The mother woke up just in time to see her son go into the water. The helicopter lifted the boy out of the water and back toward the deck. The mother saw her son come out of the water, panicked and spitting salt water and in this terrible state. She proceeded to faint for a third time.

But a moment later the helicopter hoisted the boy up and into its bay and it veered away. Then the second helicopter came into position to pick up the doctor. The doctor put on the horse collar and I stood him on the covering board to ready him to be hoisted. We gave the signal for the helicopter to hoist away. It lifted him a few feet off the deck and instead of pulling him straight up and into the bay door, it deposited him in the water up to his waist. But then it lifted him and brought him soaking wet into its belly.

The parents and fiancé of course wanted to be with the boy, but I had only one engine and was fifty miles offshore. I got on the radio and asked if there was anyone who would take the parents and fiancé into Cape May so they could be with the son. One of the boats in the tournament said they would help out, so they came over and picked them up for the long ride in. My passengers crossed over into the other boat leaving me there alone on the *What's Wrong*. I called over to the other boats again to explain that I didn't know exactly where I was or what heading I should take to get back in. Another boat responded giving me a course to get back in.

By now I was a complete nervous wreck. This was my first experience as the captain of a boat and I had already encountered things that no one should ever have to face. I was thinking that if I could only get to port safely this one time, I'd have to give some thought to whether or not I'd ever want to be the captain of a boat again. So, I headed in using the heading I had been given. It was a long, lonely and tense ride in. To make things worse, when I got about two miles off the Atlantic City Inlet, my engine gave out. This was not good. I came off the bridge and opened the engine hatch to perform the same procedure on that engine as I had on the other, twist the distributor cap, check the spark plug wires, tap on the carburetor. I climbed back up onto the bridge and tried the ignition. Nothing. I got the bright idea to try the other engine. Bingo! It fired and I was under weigh again. This time I made it all the way into the dock.

The story of *What's Wrong* made it through the fleet in no time at all. In New Jersey there was a twenty-one year old drinking age but I was only nineteen. Still, everyone wanted to buy me drinks and get me drunk and congratulate me.

In the morning, while the son stayed in the hospital and recovered, along came Momma, Pappa and the fiance onto the boat. They wanted to go fishing. I looked at them in amazement. I could not believe they were serious about this. I told them I would not take this boat out again for all the money in the world, they did not owe me anything for the two days they had hired me, and I quit. The owner fully understood and told me to take the day off and he would pay me for my time.

GUATEMALA BIG GAME FISHING
by
RON HAMLIN

In my periodic emails to my distribution list regarding fishing conditions off the coast of Guatemala, I rarely have to report that the fishing is off this week or that things have been slow. Usually it's more like "Things have been blistering hot" or "The bite is on." That's how it is for those bigger than life Pacific sails in this part of the world.

We fish out of the port of Iztapa, located on the west coast of Guatemala at latitude 13:47 North, 90:47 West. The fishing in this area is good all twelve months of the year, but the season that we fish covers the eight month period between October and May. The boat I run, *Capt. Hook*, a Carolina built forty-two foot Willis, stays pretty well booked up during that period.

It is not uncommon for us to release 2,000 sails in a season, and we have made world records for most sail fish released in one year, 2555; the most pacific sails released in one day, 75; and the most sails released on fly in one year, 432. We recently tied the world record for most releases on fly in a single day with 27. There are also a good number of marlin that make their way onto our baits, but these are by-catch and not our intended targets. We are out for those Pacific sails, good fighters, fun to catch and release, and readily available in very large quantities.

The coast of Guatemala is home to a plentiful shrimp population that moves all over the place. The bottom is sandy and there is no structure. On account of this the fish move around in search of food and we may have to hunt a different territory every day to find them. Our fishing area is vast, covering the waters from three to fifty miles offshore. But this keeps it interesting, and the abundant supply of shrimp offers a steady and ample diet for the sails. For this reason these sails congregate in this area and this adds to our hook-up rate. They also eat well and grow larger. One hundred pound sailfish are caught every day, and it's not all that unusual to land a 130 pounder. In the Atlantic this size would be a rarity.

It is a proven fact that Guatemala has the best sail fishing in the world. We know this because of the excellent record keeping we work so hard to preserve. I give a great deal of credit to Tim Choate. Tim has been the single most important person in having Guatemala recognized as one of the world's best fishing locales. He has been instrumental in organizing the tag and release program in Guatemala and Costa Rica. Because of his insistence on excellent record keeping we have been able to gauge our hook-up rates against those of other areas of the world. We have also learned what we know about migratory patterns of Pacific sails and certain marlin species through the study of these results. We post our results daily and the record is continually being updated.

We also get our share of blue, black and striped marlin, though I will be the first to admit that the angler looking exclusively for that type of game can do better in many other places throughout the world. (Just the same, we are always prepared with a good sized pitch bait just in case a marlin finds its way into our spread).

Over the years of fishing off Central America I have developed routines and habits that have proven to be successful at increasing my angler's sailfish hook up rates. Two things are central to this success: circle hooks and baits. Again, on account of the influence of Tim Choate I was one of the first captains in the area to convert to circle hooks. Our initial concern was for conservation and the good of the fishery. Had our hook up rate dropped we would have still stood by the circle hooks just because we felt we were doing something for the environment. But, as an added bonus, since 1998 when *Capt. Hook* converted to all circle hooks, we watched our hook up rate increase from 50%-55% to at least 60% and even as high as 70% with more experienced and confident anglers. At the same time we watched our gut hook rate drop by 50%. (That statistic is in part because of the use of circle hooks and part because of the drop back technique we use since the development of circle hooks). Our average catch rate today is fifteen sails per day using circle hooks compared to ten years ago when average would have been much lower, and a great day would have been twenty sails. Now twenty is considered pretty good but certainly far from great.

My bait of choice is ballyhoo which has proven over the years to be the superior bait for sailfish. While we always keep a large mackerel handy for the opportunity to pitch to a blue marlin, we have found that the ballyhoos with the 7/0 circle hooks will get the job done on them as well. On those wild days when we raise one hundred sails, we give credit to the ballyhoos.

Our rods are all Cape Fear, our reels are Shimano and Fin Nor, and our line is Suffix. Our hooks are Eagle Claw (both circle and fly), and my teasers are Softhead. In Guatemala, with the amount of action we see, it's easy to have the skirts pulled off ordinary teasers. This can not happen with Softheads. If I have two or three teasers tracking well I leave them alone. I do not believe in constantly changing them out and I also do not believe that the color of the teasers is all that important. Some boats are constantly changing out their teasers, but I believe this is more to make it look like they are trying harder than actually accomplishing something important. To me, the only important thing is how well they stay in the water and that they do not spin.

Unlike most captains, I do not continue in a straight line when I raise a fish. As soon as a fish comes into our spread I want everyone holding a line while I circle around to try to stay in the area. When one fish comes up there are usually more fish in the area and they will stay nearby if one is hooked up. This way we have a perfect shot at a double or triple header.

Circle hooks and ballyhoo can not be effective if the angler does not have the technique. On board *Capt. Hook* we teach our anglers to drop back to a count of four and lock up and begin reeling. It was the underwater research of Dr. Guy Harvey that taught us that by the count of three the fish has the bait in its mouth. We take a count of four and begin reeling so that the fish does not take the bait into its stomach. This helps to avoid the gut hook and the longer drop back count is not necessary.

Fishing on board *Capt. Hook* is intended as a fun, learning experience. When new anglers come on board we school them in our four count drop back technique, how to hold the rod and how to fight the fish. For the first day the mates will help them by hooking the fish and handing the rod over. But by the second day the angler will be on his own, holding the rod, dropping back, locking up and reeling. By learning the proper technique our anglers improve their hook up rate, avoid backlashes, and ultimately increase their enjoyment of the experience.

This is the famous forty-two foot Carolina built Willis called *Captain Hook*.
Captained by Ron Hamlin, no boat in the world today has caught and
released more billfish. *Captain Hook* charters out of Ixtapa, Guatemala.

Captain
Bart Miller

©Kevin Nakamaru

CAPTAIN BART MILLER

Bart Miller's love for fishing started at four years old while fishing in creeks and progressing to lakes in northern California. Trout of various types were his primary targets. As a pre-teen Bart moved to southern California where he changed over from fresh water to ocean fishing from the beach, piers, and boats. His early catches included sardines, smelt, herring, Tom cods, croaker, mackerel, bonehead bonita, perch and halibut. All of these species were very plentiful albeit seasonal, but southern California and Mexico had something going all the time.

Upon reaching his teens, Bart progressed to fishing the party boats half day and full day, catching barracuda, white sea bass, yellow tail, halibut, snapper, rock cod, ling cod and albacore. This exciting period of fishing began around 1950. Bart was living in the Ocean Park - Santa Monica - Venice area of southern California. Other hot spot fishing destinations were out of San Pedro, Newport Beach, San Clemente, San Diego, Baja California, Ensenada, Cabo San Lucas, and San Felipe.

Bart's fishing addiction progressed to big game fishing by 1964 while he was residing in Hawaii crewing on a charter boat out of Kailua-Kona. In 1965 he decided to make fishing his career by becoming a Captain. He had moved up the scale from small fish to marlin, tuna, wahoo and dolphin. He was fully hooked, spending his days from sunrise to sunset fishing for the most majestic fish in the world oceans, from an address known as Kona, Hawaii. Not too shabby! This early period in big game fishing was the golden era; fishing out of Kona is a fishermen's dream: big fish, and lots of fish, and great weather.

Bart started out by learning a lot his first year crewing for a couple of different Captains. His first boat named *Adelante* was a wooden Hawaiian high bowed Sampan with a single diesel engine. Not much of a boat by today's standard but good enough for him to catch eighty-seven blue marlin during a single season. This feat became a new local record for the most marlin ever caught during a single season.

Bart broke his own record by catching 100 plus blue marlin, a feat that he accomplished in a single season a couple of times. Bart once again won top boat honors by winning the coveted Henry Chee top captain trophy during the 1967 Hawaiian International Billfish Tournament. Captain Miller won this same tournament again in 1975 setting a record for the most points ever scored in this prestigious event.

In all, Bart had five boats in Kona through the years 1965-1994 when he left the islands. His last boat was the legendary Merritt boat *Black Bart*. That boat has a different owner now and still charters in Kona. It is now called *Huntress*.

In 1968 he visited Fiji and Samoa, fishing 1969 in New Zealand's Bay of Islands, and in 1970 he fished Australia's Great Barrier Reef where the boat he crewed on caught two black marlin over 1000 pounds.

Fishing in Kona continued to improve for Bart, winning more tournaments and setting records during the Hawaiian International Allison Yellowfin Tuna tournaments. He had back-to-back wins 1974 and 1975 winning the 1975 tournament with a smashing score that exceeded his nearest competition by 2,000 points, a record that has never been equaled.

In 1983 Bart caught his first Pacific blue marlin grander. It weighted 1,265 pounds and was caught on live bait, a six pound aku.

In 1984 he caught his second Pacific blue marlin grander. That was the famous 1,656 pounder that was the largest blue marlin ever caught in Kona and the second largest blue marlin ever caught on rod and reel. The lure that caught this famous fish was hand made by Bart himself.

Bart spent the 1994 and 1995 seasons in Madeira, Portugal where he caught many good sized marlin and four over a grand each. In 1996 Bart fished the Bahamas Billfish Championships winning trophies and other tournament prizes.

Captain Miller's fishing travels have taken him to far away places like St. Thomas, Virgin Islands, Costa Rica, Tahiti, Fiji, Samoa, New Zealand, Australia, Bahamas, Madeira, Mexico, Hawaii, Texas, Florida and California. He says that each of these destinations filled his soul with rich experiences. They were special times shared with special people.

Today Bart is the CEO of Black Bart International, which is a life style, up-scale custom tackle store in Riviera Beach of the Palm Beaches, Florida. In that tackle boutique is a showcase of Bart's history through photos and collections of memorabilia from his big game fishing history. Many of the products showcased in this unique store are Captain Bart Miller's original designs found no where else.

THE STORY OF THE 1,656
by
BART MILLER

I would like to invite you aboard my sleek fishing machine for the catch of a lifetime. Notice the large cockpit and superb tackle. There is none finer. If you need to use the head, it's forward on the port side. You're welcome on the bridge and, if you care to brave the climb, in the tower as well. Come on up.

The charter today is Mr. Rankin Smith, Jr. and his buddy Gary Merriman, both of Atlanta, Georgia. Junior's father, Rankin Smith, Sr., used to fish with me. He was quite the man. He would talk investments, insurance and other forms of high finance with me and I would talk thermoclines, ocean currents and big fish with him. What a pair we were! Rankin owned the Life of Georgia Insurance Company and the Atlanta Falcons football team, and he loved big game fishing. I miss him, as he was one of the characters I've met in my life of whom I was most fond. But this day my guest is his offspring, Rankin Jr.

It's 8:00 o'clock in the morning of March 16, 1984 and we're headed toward Otech Buoy, north of the harbor. We're cruising at twenty-five knots and the run takes about one hour. The plan is to catch live aku (skipjack) and put them out for bait, hoping to trade one for a nice ahi or blue marlin. I chat with junior along the way as I did his dad before him. He tells me he just bought a new boat, a sixty foot Hatteras. When I asked him the name of his new lady he smiled and said, "*Pocket Change.*" It seems the apple does not fall far from the tree. Junior's friend, Gary, looked a lot like the movie character Indiana Jones. A little later in the day Gary would prove just how much he was like the amazing Mr. Jones.

We approached the buoy and I circled it to check the current and look for aku on the surface. Several local skiff fishermen signaled to let me know it was dead there, so we changed plans. Junior and Gary said, "Do whatever you feel is best, only make sure the end result is a big marlin." So I put out a team of lures tuned specifically for big ones and started trolling south. Over the years, lure trolling had become my favorite game. I had designed each lure in the pattern for a specific position. I climbed into the tower to help Dominic, my mate, set them properly on each wake. After tweaking the lures I returned to the flybridge to check the depth recorder. Eleven hundred fathoms was a breeze for this machine and, under the best of conditions, it would pump out 1,500 fathoms. I found some nice current slicks in eight hundred fathoms and I favored this depth for the zone I was working. In recent days, fishing had been deathly slow and the radio was quiet. I scanned the horizon with my Zeiss binoculars looking for birds, dolphin splashes, floating objects, anything that might indicate fish; but there was nothing to see. When conditions are like this, it is wise to buckle down to basics, make yourself comfortable, but always be ready for anything. Make every effort to stay positive, even if the effort seems futile.

The eight hundred fathom curve kept me away from the other boats, but they weren't catching anything either. Once I got even with the Grounds, I chose to work the deep drops in that area; trolling from 500 fathoms to 1,500 fathoms. It was a gray day with a mild chop under light winds. The lures were a pleasure to watch. I was relaxed and time was standing still - a survival trick captains learn or their nerves would leap out and bite them.

AN APPARITION APPEARS

It was getting on 2:00 PM and the autopilot was set on a 160 degree course. The depth was 750 fathoms and the gray backdrop magnified the white trail jetting off the back end of each lure. It was a showy, aggressive pattern tailing down sea at eight knots. It was then I saw something the likes of which I had never seen before and have not seen since. She was just there, as if she had magically appeared, moving perpendicular to my pattern and taking aim at the lure in the short rigger position. The great marlin was offering me an incredible view as she literally surfed on her belly toward the lure that displayed no fear at her approach. She looked almost mechanical, more like a fine sculpture in bronze than an actual living creature. She showed so much of herself that I was left in awe. Great fish usually sneak in, attack and disappear, and experienced captains know you never get a full side view like this.

My eyes were taking mental photographs as they traced her sideways, up and down. This was the fish I had waited for all my life; the one anglers and captains worldwide would die for. My first guess at her weight was computed in a second at over 1,300 pounds. In a flash, I was out of the helm chair, facing aft with both hands on the throttles behind me. I was calm and steady, like a marksman taking aim, ready to squeeze the trigger. I had done all the knee-knocking, heart-pounding crap years before and those days were long behind me. Loud and clear I yelled out, "Right rigger - BIG FISH!" No sooner did the words leave my lips and she was gone. She never touched the lure.

My first thought was, "She'll be back." The lures kept pumping in the wake doing exactly what they must to peak the prey-drive of a monster like this. I stayed put, hands on the throttles, waiting, believing that she would return. I pondered whether I should turn back or hold course. I held course and the seconds turned into minutes as my eyes strained along with my belief that she would be back for a second shot.

Dominic appeared below me in the cockpit and asked what I was sounding off about. I could not believe that I was the only one who had witnessed this magnificent sight. Junior and Gary popped to attention and asked, "How big?"

"Well over 1,000 pounds!" I remarked. "The largest marlin I have ever seen." Everyone settled back as if to say, "Yeah, sure." They showed little concern over my excitement.

I was pissed and could not understand why the great fish did not attack. I left the Grounds and headed further north and out to sea. This set was called the 'Lighthouse-Cinder Cone' run, one of the favorites of local captains. I completed the run when the depth recorder indicated we crossed into 1,000 fathoms and turned the bow toward Kaieve Point and the Hilton Hotel. While on this run back in 700 fathoms she appeared again, a full forty minutes after the first showing.

This time I got an even better view of her, and I wasn't alone. Everyone onboard saw her clearly and was mesmerized! Was this the same fish? It couldn't be an another one that big! But it really didn't matter. She was back and on the same lure, posing in the same mechanical manner, only this time coming more from the quarter with greater speed and authority. This time she meant business.

HOOK UP

Gary was ready, as Junior had told him to take the first fish. Once again the marlin faded away, but as before, I believed in my bones she would return. Damn her though, why is she doing this to me? Come back and show yourself. Bite and hook-up! That is what you are supposed to do. I held the course for another fifteen minutes and she came back again, this time like a submarine, water pouring off her back, her mighty sword moving from side-to-side with each undulation of her flanks. She was settled deep in the water, approaching fast and furious from directly behind the very lure she had declined twice before.

My hands were resting on the throttles as I enjoyed a calm I had never known before. Her head rolled to the right, her mouth was open, I saw jaws shut down tight on the lure, I watched as she dove and turned with explosive authority. I pulled the throttles all the way back, shifted into reverse and, with not a second wasted, backed down hard sending the rest of the lures toward the bow and beyond.

I heard Dominic yell, "Hold on, the lures need to be reeled in!" But I wasn't going to fall for that one. I could have cared less about the other lures with this fish on. Gary was buckled in the fighting chair looking like a light heavyweight prizefighter. The 130 pound line was being dumped off the powerful Zane Grey reel like I had never seen before and the stump-puller rod was arched and doing its damage. All the support systems were ready and I was pushing the Merritt in reverse, water splashing high over the transom, flooding the teak cockpit sole. Two hundred yards of line was gone in a flash and the fish was coming to the surface to show off; exactly what I wanted her to do. I spun the boat on a dime, slamming one transmission into reverse and the other forward, swinging the rudder hard over and then pushing the throttles to sunset. The wheel was turned back to center, both gears were pushed ahead and we were parallel to the fish getting line back on the reel as we paced her. The high capacity bilge pumps were blowing their load, but we were more than holding our own against the brute force of this mighty creature.

KEEP THE PRESSURE ON

Being only men we don't know the true capabilities of these black and silver acrobats. But I knew this fish was angry and she liked neither the pull of the line on the side of her head nor the proximity of her tormentors. I pressed her even harder because I wanted her up and out of the water in a great jump, filling her air sacks and tiring her great muscles. This was how we would defeat her. We were very close when she decided it was show time. God what a sight as she powered her way through the choppy sea leaving the water for the sky! Her initial slow motion posing changed to a gyration, a blur of vibrating muscles and swatting tail. She reached heights that I had only seen in much smaller billfish. Her fury, grace and speed are indescribable yet as vivid as if the encounter happened yesterday! Her temper flared and she wanted to crush everything in her path. Jump after jump, she kept at it as if there would be no end, while I backed down on her even harder, closing the distance. The pressure was getting to Gary, sweating in the chair, but it was obvious he was not going to give an inch.

Six high capacity bilge pumps were set on manual trying to evacuate the seawater from the boat. We had been backing down in hot pursuit and taking on water, when she decided to sound. This is when the fight gets down and dirty. It would become a power game and we had to let her run against the drag, which was set at about forty-five pounds, as she dove. I wanted her to slow down, to give in just a little, so that we could get the drag up to sixty pounds. The increased pressure would encourage her to surface again.

If you are ever in such a battle, then you must work hard to redirect a diving blue marlin. You want to keep a big one as close to the surface as possible. Black marlin that dive usually return to the surface quickly, but that is not case with blues. They will dive to incredible depths, dog it, and eventually die there. When this happens you have two very difficult problems: first, how to lift that much dead weight from the depths, and second, the worry of getting shark bit. Your single-minded goal must be to stay as close as possible to a big blue. For every inch she takes, try to get back two. Be decisive and remain resolute. It took me years to learn how to fight big blue marlin and there is just no question about it - if you lose control, your chances of winning go with it.

This great blue lady was now taking us on a journey further out to sea. As she slowed, we were finally able to increase drag to seventy pounds and, for brief moments, even higher. She would respond with extra force as if to say, "You will not tame me, you will never see me die!" This course of action was working, but I realized we needed another man in the cockpit, someone special, a really good wireman. Dominic would be the gaffman, but he just was not up to wiring a fish of this size. I got on the radio and asked for back up and several boats responded.

The *No Problem*, a 43 foot Merritt, was nearby and volunteered their gaffman, Fran. I knew him to be one of the best, so we made the transfer, the two Merritts going bow to bow. We now had a wireman, gaffman, helmsman, and angler - the team was complete.

Wasting no time, I pushed the boat closer and closer to the fish. There was no need to turn and chase anymore as the fight had changed from moving offshore to the fish pulling in all directions, including concentric circles, none of which were difficult for the boat to follow. The fight was now like a dance and it was up to me to follow and still keep plenty of pressure on the head of this great fish. Fran was doing an excellent job coaching the angler, telling him just how much drag to use, when to work, when to pause. We kept the heat on the fish and Gary was showing no signs of collapse. I asked him regularly how he was faring and he always smiled and said, "I'm fine, thank you."

THE END GAME

After two hours of intense give-and-take the fish was beginning to show signs of tiring. Fran put on his hefty gloves, wet them and began performing shoulder and deep breathing exercises, preparing for the final test. My job required I keep the boat at just the right distance from the fish, doing everything in my power to give an advantage to the wireman. We could see the marlin quite clearly now, her head going away from the stern, her massive body undulating as we backed down and closed the gap. Every time we applied more pressure she would swing from port to starboard and back, repeating this motion over and over, making it difficult for me to place her in a set position for the gaff. She was easily sixteen feet long and snaking from side to side with incredible grace.

The bottoms of my feet were burning from being planted in one spot for so long. My elbows were stiff for the same reason, but this was endured as I maintained total concentration on the fish and the boat. The radio was ablaze with conversation about the battle. The other captains in the fleet were well aware it was drawing to a close by the way the boat was being handled.

Fran was still stretching and breathing hard, looking for all the world like a fighter about to enter the ring for the first round. The time came, and as the fish swam within reach, Fran took a quick aggressive and powerful wrap. Just as quickly the fish shook its mighty head shaking the wireman to his bones, causing him to release. The power of this marlin was enough to rip body parts off if not treated with great care and respect.

Things settle down once again and Fran reached for the leader a second time, but he could not get enough slack to lay a wrap, and I could not get any closer to the fish to assist him. This was the point in the fight that the tension was highest, because this is when the unexpected is most likely to occur, and I was not about to lose this fish.

Fran signaled that she was coming up to jump so I pushed the throttles down and gave her everything we had. Fran grabbed handfuls of wraps and, in a flash, the fish was in reach of the gaffs. It was at that moment I knew everything was going to come together. Dominic reached over the enormous shoulders and placed the first gaff deep in the big fish. Junior placed the second gaff and

Fran reached out and placed the third, pinning the huge marlin to the port side of the boat. I came down off the bridge and placed a fourth gaff in the head, tying a half hitch to secure the bill that was as big as a man's leg.

I quickly thanked everyone on board. Gary, Junior, Fran, Dominic, each did an incredible job as this was the most difficult fish I had ever fought. It took two hours and twenty minutes of intense pressure to subdue her, and getting her into the boat took another twenty minutes. Her tail was seven feet from tip to tip and had to be left outside of the tuna door for the ride home. The radio was crackling with congratulations. I was still in shock as I looked at the massive fish that filled my cockpit. I went to the tower so that I could be alone and get a better look. I could not believe my eyes, knowing this was the largest blue to ever be weighed in Kona. My feelings at the time were uncomfortable. I wasn't proud of what I had accomplished; yet I wasn't ashamed, either. I was simply and soulfully sorry that this beautiful creature was no longer alive.

Word spread via the coconut express that my boat would be coming to Kailua Pier to weigh a very big marlin. Never had I seen so many people gathered on the pier or running down the streets. There was a carnival atmosphere in the air. A long rope was placed around the tail of fish, the other end went to the pier attendants who tied it off to a cleat. I then engaged the gears and powered ahead in order to get her massive body out of the boat for weigh in. The weighmaster announced that this great Pacific blue marlin weighed an astonishing 1,656 pounds. At that moment, another captain and personal friend asked me why I wasn't jumping for joy. I assured him that I was very happy and deeply satisfied, but if he wanted to see me do a jig on the dock then the fish would have to weigh a ton. **Papa**

TU TU
by
BART MILLER

Two mysterious hours passed in our slow motion tug of war game with Tu Tu. There were brief moments when I could make out the marlin clearly; blood still trailing ominously from its gills, but the color had changed to a light watermelon red that faded quickly in our wake. The great fish seemed to be getting weaker, bleeding out, probably the reason we were able to stay attached to her. The eighty pound tackle was nothing more than ultra light tackle to this fish. The crew and my anglers could occasionally make out the great shadow at the other end of the line, but they could not get as clear a picture as I could from my vantage point on the bridge.

Once again, the questions were raised from the deck. "How big? Is it a grander?" they demanded. I knew that soon enough they'd be able to make up their own minds, however their persistence spurred me to finally blurt out, "If you chopped off its fucking head and weighed it, that part would weigh a thousand pounds!"

There was stunned silence from the cockpit. No one said a word. The realization of what was at the other end of the line left crew and angler alike in a near trance. We worked the fish closer, and the angle on the line decreased. We all sensed the same thing; we were going to see her; she might even jump. The fish was a mere forty feet away.

When the mass of her enormous body raised from the sea in a display that brought her out of the water to her anal fin, pink blood washed from her mouth and the muscles in her flanks rippled and flexed as she fell back, splashing a geyser of water in all directions. Her monstrous head thrashed from side to side, and she blew out her huge stomach, disgorging its contents. Reef fish, large and small, were strewn over the surface and floating every direction. The amazing volume of partially digested fish created a large oil slick, and gross stench permeated our surroundings. This experience was so incredible I never mentioned it before because I felt no one would ever believe me.

After seeing the great fish, no one on board doubted what we had to deal with. This fish was twenty-five feet long and we had it on an eighty pound rig, deployed for 200 pound tuna. A strange new fear came over me unlike any I'd ever known before. I was afraid of making a critical mistake and losing this incredible opportunity. I'd been hunting for a 'tonner' and I now had one far larger hooked up near my boat. This was the realization of my quest for a truly great marlin. Over the years, I'd worked hard to learn all I could about these fish, their movements and migrations, the ways to appeal to the very biggest that lived in this infinite water. I'd experienced thousands of battles, some lost, some won, and understood the best attitude to carry into the fight was one neither positive nor negative. Never wish things to happen, accept your limitations and try to simply stay in step with whatever occurs. Stay mentally focused and learn to react to each move the fish makes and avoid mistakes by being sure your gear and your crew are up to any challenge that presents itself. Put yourself in the right places at the right times of day and use all your skills and experience to tip the scales in your favor... but enough business philosophy.

It was now four hours since we first hooked Tu Tu, the honored grandmother. The fight had changed; she was no longer headed out to sea. We were forced to follow her back to where she first took the bait meant for tuna only one fifteenth her remarkable size. We were going back to the sacred fishing grounds off Milolli. Her shadow was still visible like an apparition some forty feet under the surface of the clear, blue water. We lost some line as she kicked her massive tail, but she always came back and settled in at the same distance, just beyond our ability to reach her. We could watch, but we couldn't touch! The frustration was overwhelming as we knew she would also destroy any preconceived notion of how big blue marlin can grow.

We were back at the B Buoy, and the fish headed directly for one of the commercial skiffs. Trying to let the commercial fishermen know I was hooked to a big marlin, I waved frantically at the fisherman in the stern. He took a moment to acknowledge our presence, but the look on his face told the story... "You're on your own!" I realized that we'd get no leeway from this busy village fisherman. Fortunately, at the last minute the fish turned and avoided his boat. If my taught line had crossed that of the commercial tuna hand liner, then mine would have been cut off, no doubt about it.

I was tired of the game of 'dog walking man'. The singularly unspectacular fight was bordering on monotony. I began to think that if I had only put out my "stump puller" outfit, an unlimited-class rod with a 12/0 Zane Gray reel loaded with 130 pound Dacron and a 700 pound leader tied to a 12/0 double strength forged hook, I could apply enough drag to finish the fish. It certainly wouldn't diminish the magnitude of the accomplishment, and the heavier gear might let us turn her head and lift her to the boat. Damned if we weren't stuck trying to do the job with the wrong tools. It forced me to walk a tight rope, staying with the fish, applying only as much pressure as the eighty allowed, hoping we could hold her until she bled out, hoping the sharks didn't home in on her blood trail before it was over. I counted my blessings. At least she stayed in easy range, and was visible. If she slugged it out deep and died there, we'd never be able to lift her lifeless body to the surface with this outfit.

We were now six and a half hours into the fight. Suddenly, the angle on the line changed, and she came to the surface. I reversed hard, the gaff was lifted from the deck, the wireman readied himself and the angler pumped harder. This was it, the moment of truth we'd been waiting and working to achieve. She was about to slide up the starboard side, her massive black eye looking tired to the point of appearing drugged. I slid in and out of gear ever so carefully, trying to let her finally be transferred from the rod to the wireman's gloved hands.

At that exact moment, a flood of positive energy coursed through my consciousness. "We're going to catch her! She'll easily weigh some 3,000 pounds! She's twenty-five feet long!" My brain almost screamed in my ears…. "My God, she's twice the size of the 1656!" How can any man be so lucky? The photos that will be taken, the stories that will be told! Too bad it wasn't a more impressive fight, just a huge fish that finally bled to death.

Suddenly, there she was, lying on her side, her colors still vivid. Broad bands of copper hues, the jet-black back, blues and purples and a pearl-white belly all shown like she was lit from within. The wireman stretched out over the gunwales, reaching for the leader when inexplicably his posture changed. He turned his head away from the fish and looked up at me with abject disappointment in his eyes. He was trying to tell me something, but all he could do was mouth the words; no sound passed his lips. I looked at the great marlin and watched in horror as Tu Tu weakly paddled her massive tail ever so slightly, slowly propelling her huge mass down and out of view. She was gone, forever!

I bounded from the flybridge, reaching the fighting chair in several steps. I grabbed the line, which had broken near the rod tip, I inspected the line at the break, no chafe or wear was visible. Bryan, who had so valiantly fought the great fish for all these hours, sat heart broken, literally hurt with the grief borne of defeat. The crew was disgusted to the point of being sick, both mentally and physically. There was nothing to say, nothing that would have changed the moment or relieved the private sense of hell we all felt.

The crew recovered rapidly, having fought and lost before. For Bryan, it was another story. He'd made a mistake, one we'd learn about later when we reviewed the battle. He had put his strong thumbs on the spool at that last moment in an effort to put just a little more pressure on the fish to get it to the wireman. He could never have known the little extra would cost us all, not only a fish of a lifetime, but a fish of a million life times, a fish only a privileged few would even glimpse, never mind hook and fight.

I returned to the helm and pushed the throttles of the *Black Bart* up to cruise, pointing the boat toward home. It was late, and it would be dark before we made the harbor at Kailua Kona. The breeze freshened, like it had early in the morning when the day was fresh with promise. Then I laughed out loud, not so loud that it could be heard in the cockpit over the drumming of the big diesels, and smiled. I was remembering the thought that danced through my head, as we had the great fish alongside the boat. One in particular I could literally see in my mind's eye just before we lost her - the image of our pictures being taken along side the triple grander, the flash bulbs brightly dancing. The cool Hawaiian night and fresh trade winds calmed me for what was not to be.

EPILOGUE

While you might doubt the size of the marlin recounted in this very true story, I can assure you there are specimens swimming the oceans of the world that far exceed any that have been brought to boat by hook and line. The 1,656 pound Pacific blue marlin I caught in 1984 was aged by biologists at thirty years. This was determined by analyzing the annular rings of the otoliths, small bones found in the skull that provide the accurate method of determining age. It is believed that blue marlin can live to be fifty years of age.

As a result of many discussions with biologists who study the great ocean predators, I firmly believe not just age, but genetics play an important part in determining the potential size of each large female blue marlin. Some are genetically predisposed to grow larger and faster than their sisters. In conclusion, the largest marlin that I have seen caught over the years, mine as well as others, had their stomachs full of deep water sea life. This to me indicates that they probably spend the majority of their senior years feeding deep where clouds of easy prey are abundant. We encountered Tu Tu using a live aku fished down twenty fathoms, probably the upper limits of her deep water foraging habits.

Maybe some day Tu Tu will be caught and smash the all tackle record. She is certainly there for the taking.

Great Fishing & Aloha,

Capt. Bart Miller.

TUNA SAMURAI
by
BART MILLER

The year was 1974 and my new Merritt, *Black Bart*, had just arrived in Honolulu. We had made it just in time to be dry docked and readied for the first Hawaiian International Allison Yellowfin Tuna Tournament to be held at Pokai Bay. Fifty teams from around the islands had signed up for this tournament. This was a real plus for me as it would allow me to secure a good shake down cruise, still keeping me in the proximity of excellent marine service in Honolulu if we needed it.

My team, the Japanese team of Miake Island, Japan, qualified for the title 'International Team'. Team captain, Shigeyuki Tachibana, and his friends would be my anglers and sponsors for this event. Capt. Tachibana, whose name means Wild Orange in Japanese, is the most intense angler and personality I had ever met. Known as Shige by his friends, Tachibana literally considered himself some kind of modern-day Samurai. For him, losing was simply out of the question. He would boldly say, "Losing is not an option." I liked this kind of attitude, especially in a sponsor and angler like him. He was a fierce warrior of big game fishing. I had always considered myself an intense person, but when placed alongside of Shige, I was overshadowed by his defiance and optimism. (Shige said the same of me.)

I had never fished the fertile waters off the Wainaie coast of Oahu and was really looking forward to this new challenge. I checked with the top local captains to find where the local tuna hotspots were. Most of the free information came back telling me to fish the 1,000 fathom curve inside the lee of the island, straight out front of Pokai Bay. I was told to just stay in that zone and eventually the ahi would come right to me. I intended to follow this strategy for the five day tournament.

What I did not like about the plan was that most likely all the captains who said that this zone was the hot spot would be fishing that very same area. When fishing for tuna and trying to win a tournament, I prefer to find a hot spot just for myself, a place where I am not sharing tuna. This, of course, is easier said than done.

Tachibana and his interpreter quizzed me the night before the tournament. They checked all tackle, mostly hooks and tuna lures. We had plastic boxes each filled with six lures, hooks and leaders, all ready to fish. Our spare lure program numbered at least sixty lures. We would not be doing any re-rigging along the way, so we made certain that we had more lures, hooks and leaders ready to fish than we would require for the entire week.

The Japanese style was to fish hard, fish well and waste no time; leader and lure would stay with the tuna after it was boated. The word 'serious' does not adequately describe the method a Japanese angler applies to himself; 'perfect', 'extreme' or 'intense' would be a better descriptive.

A SAMURAI'S PREPARATION

When the morning of the tournament arrived, everyone was doing his and her special thing, whatever that might be. The diesel engines were all humming and ticking; the smell was that of tournament time. This is when a calm washed over me that told me that I was ready. I became a very private person at these times and I did not like to socialize when the start was near. Tachibana liked this in me. This morning he bought deluxe Japanese breakfast for all, and had also purchased Japanese lunches for our team. My crew consisted of brothers Dirk and Bart, and Uki, a Japanese crew member supplied by Mr. Tachibana.

The competitors and boats were all lined up for the start. I loved the feel of wood and the power of the great diesels. As the words came across the radio to start fishing, I eased the throttles ahead bringing the RPM up to thirty knots cruising speed, fully two to three times as fast as most of the other boats in the 1973 Hawaiian fleet. My new Merritt reached the 1,000-fathom curve shortly after the start, ahead of all the other boats. This was my first use of a tuna tower. Small pitches and rolls that were barely felt by men with sea legs when standing on the bridge or in the cockpit were magnified many times at the thirty foot extension of the tuna tower. It's a mathematical geometric progression that causes the top of those towers to swing pronouncedly to and fro even in fairly calm seas. And I knew that the tower is where I would perch throughout the better part of the tournament.

My skilled crew worked feverishly to set all the lines in tournament fashion. We fished four eighty pound rigs. The lures were all mother of pearl and abalone shell, lead-weighted to swim just beneath the surface. The lure size choices were assorted six, seven and nine inch. Our leaders were 300 pound test. We also had leaders of 200 pound test standing by in case the tuna were shy. The hooks were double-hook rigs set at 180 degrees. Our hook sizes were assorted 7/0 and 8/0.

The lines were positioned and tournament ready. There was high anticipation aboard by all. Those feelings waned as the fresh morning air turned into the bright light of noon, then later in the day turned into afternoon.

"Stop fishing, stop fishing!" echoed across the radio, transmitting the end of the first day's tuna fishing. Two ahi were caught this day by the fleet of fifty boats and they were small ones which weighed in at 130 and 137 pounds. Not a good day for most. The weather had been balmy and the seas were flat. These were not good conditions for tuna fishing. Brisk winds and steady currents make for more optimal tuna fishing.

My crew, Dirk and Bart, paced themselves and were waiting for the opportunity that would strip line from our reels and empower our spirits. Disappointing as it was, we did not have a strike or any other opportunity for the next four long days. The seas continued to stay calm; the normal tradewinds had vanished, as had the ahi. Tournament competition had given way to parties that lasted late into each night.

Friday was the last day of the tournament. We had endured five long and arduous days, with no birds, no bait, and no fishing clues. I was blistered from the heat and long hours of nothingness. My Japanese team had not given up nor had the crew; all we needed was a good bite and we could still win this tournament. That was all anyone needed. The tournament glory was open to all as the few ahi that had been caught were small, each under 200 pounds. Stop fishing and the end of the tournament was 4 PM. I looked at my watch as I had so many times that week. The time was 3:15 PM.

My view from the tower was almost bird-like. It was a place where tuna fishermen live while fishing tuna. I could see each of the four lures swimming just inches below the surface, their pearl shell heads glowing. The entire package fish-like; each lure carving its own path, a temptation that no big fish could possibly resist. We were ready, willing and able . . . then it happened. I saw what I had so patiently been waiting for: ahi on the flat lines. I could see they were both going to bite. They were big, fat Allison yellowfin tuna, each one over 200 pounds. Allison tuna are bomb-like in shape, with colors of emerald green, black, blue, gold, pearl pink and creamy white, and are painted with the brightest yellow fins in the world. I will never tire viewing these deliciously perfect denizens of the deep. I could taste victory with this hungry vision, and I whistled loudly and yelled out, "Ahi on the flat lines!"

The strikes came almost simultaneously, first one, then the other. There is no mistaking a tuna strike from any other species; the positive downward pull is uncommonly perfect. Yes! Both of our anglers were dealing with screaming reels. The rigger lines were cleared quickly and I was moving my new Merritt in reverse, trying to help the anglers not waste any energy on line that did not need to be dumped. I called in a double ahi hook-up to the tournament committee boat. I could almost feel the frustration of the fifty teams in the tournament trying to deal with my good fortune. Our lazy blue days had now turned bright red. We were filled with the thrill of action, and ultimately satisfaction.

Victory was ours to hold high as we raced back to port. Our two ahi flags whipped proudly in the Hawaiian breezes. I looked down from the bridge at the two tuna being washed down and covered with crushed ice. I will never forget the beaming face of Tachibana, the Tuna Warrior. This was what he had come for, a Samurai victory. We shook each other's hand, we bowed and vowed to meet each other next year to defend our title at Pokai Bay.

THE AHI TOURNAMENT OF 1975

We met often and worked late into the evening to be ready for the 1975 ahi tournament. Our plastic tackle boxes and trays had the finest collection of handmade tuna lures, leaders and hook rigs one could ever imagine. They were all Japanese, perfect in every aspect. Such a mother lode of fishing gear I had never seen, not even in my wildest dreams. We were ready to meet the challenge.

Black Bart and I had bonded well and, best of all, I had the same crew with me for this event as the previous year. Several days before the tournament we took the Merritt to Honolulu, then to Pokai Bay via Kona. The trade winds were howling, creating conditions that showed promising signs of a hot tuna tournament.

Tachibana met us at the docks while we were washing the boat down and getting ready for his Japanese team. Although he was a hard-nose task commander, he also was a charming sort of Samurai. He knew when to smile, when to furrow his brow, and how to get action from his team members. He invited me to the captains' meeting, knowing that I would turn him down. He smiled and left.

"See you in the morning, Bart," followed with a, "don't worry, you are ready, Captain."

Most everyone had gone to the hotel for the captains' meeting and buffet. The harbor was quiet, just the way I liked it. This was a time to meditate and prepare for the next five hard days of competition. There was no turning back now.

I decided to hunt down a meal within walking distance, and soon located a bar and cafe by the name of Mother's Place. Little did I know that when I went through those doors my whole week of fishing, and my life as I knew it would be altered beyond any imagination I possessed. The place was empty except for three men drinking beer and talking at the bar. They were talking about ahi and their location. But these were not tournament fishermen, these were commercial longline fishermen. I knew this because they looked different and they were talking of tuna caught by the tons.

I seldom drink, but something told me to nestle up to the bar and order a beer. I made conversation with these men. They knew something that I did not, the exact position of the tuna I was about to hunt for the next week. I could not believe it, just three commercial fishermen and me. All of this information was available just a short walking distance from the harbor. My anti-social tournament behavior was about to pay off big time. Of the three men talking, one looked quite a bit different than the other two. He was dressed in finer clothes and had a leadership quality, tone and style that was immediately evident.

I introduced myself to the man doing most of the talking. I told him who I was, where I lived, and told him of the tuna tournament about to start the next morning. He told me that his name was Mr. De Silva, and he said he owned some longline boats. He said that he flies his private plane and spots tuna for his commercial fleet and spoke of large schools of ahi forming on the windward side not too very far offshore. He also said that he had not seen tuna fishing this good in years. I promptly bought my new friends several rounds of beers. We talked of fishing, his style and mine, and he offered to lead me to the tuna if I ventured into his area while he was spotting. "You will see us, my boats are colored blue and I will be flying near to them," he said.

The zone he was talking about was at least forty miles from the Pokai Bay start line, and was most assuredly not in the lee of the island. Quite the contrary, it was directly facing and into the trade winds. I asked De Silva what the weather had been like.

"Good tuna weather," he proclaimed, "but not good if you are a man in a boat." He shrugged his shoulders and added, "When you get into the tuna, you will see many frigate birds gathering. I will be like one of them, flying, excited, and hungry. When I see you and your Merritt, I'll buzz you and then circle over the good areas, the places where the ahi are feeding. You'll have lots of fun and win the tournament."

We had a good time talking, but I was nervous with anticipation. What I had just learned, if it was true, and there was no reason to believe it wasn't, would set me apart from the rest of the fleet, and at worse give me a great head start. I went back to my boat with every fiber in me turned on and ready to go ahi fishing. Sleep came with much difficulty that anxious night before the tournament; my crew slept better, not knowing what I had discovered in the bar that evening.

Tachibana showed up early as expected with Japanese breakfast and lunch. I could read in his face that he knew I knew something. Since his English was less than desirable and my plan was based around drinking in a bar with three guys I had never met before, I figured I best keep my mouth shut and just go for it.

Start fishing began at 8 AM. I was curious how many boats would head for the north shore, as I had planned to. There was a definite lee side, and then there was the north shore. I made the turn at Kaiena Point and headed straight into the massive and unforgiving seas. The winds were thirty knots and gusting, small craft warnings were posted and the seas were ranging from six to fifteen feet. I looked back and saw that no boats were following. Lucky me, I had these killer seas all to myself.

I had to get into the tower because I could not see anything for the wind and spray which was exploding just beneath the foot stand in the tower. My crew knew to batten down all hatches, and secure all items that otherwise would be tossed around. They also knew that this day would be no picnic.

I turned *Black Bart* around down seas just long enough to climb into the tower. The lesson I had learned the previous year about the violent gyrations, the thrust and torque the tower would make, became clear to me immediately upon my arrival to its uppermost point. What I experienced in the tower was a rude awakening, at first I was being tossed and slammed around like a Raggedy Anne doll. My aluminum stilts that perched me high above the sea now seemed less alluring and more life threatening until I jury-rigged a harness that worked like a safety belt of sorts, aiding me in staying onboard. All the while the wild sea was trying to throw me off like a bucking bull sheds his rider at a rodeo. There was no mystery. I knew I was coming apart at the seams, the physical destruction and constant abuse was just part of the big game I must endure, regardless of the consequences, discomfort, pain, or other orthopedic failures being tested to the fullest. The sea has many faces, not all of them peaceful, playful, or fun. To know the sea is to respect her, all the while you love her and your reward is a good ride from time to time.

Soon enough the Samurai smiles and macho attitude were replaced with mouths full of vomit and spine-bending heaves while all the time trying to hide in the head. Of course each left the crime scene with plenty of clues belched over every surface, ceilings, bulkheads, deck and the unflushed head. Then came the very serious concern they each held for their very lives. They later admitted a fear of drowning and being attacked by sharks.

"Mind over matter, mind over matter," is the thought that permeated my brain. And then it all became so clear. We had a tournament to win, a title to defend. Now the pain had become secondary, there were bigger matters to deal with. My mind had gone to an 'other worldly' place, but it had not abandoned me completely. I risked boat, life, and limb, for this obsessive/compulsive act of competition. I have never experienced anything before or since quite like it. The crew later revealed that they had serious concerns as to my sanity. They also said that Mr. Tachibana and his guests feared for their lives, and were quite ill.

As for me, I just prayed to reach through and past one wave at a time. Often I thought of quitting. It was just too much to endure, trying to get to the zone where De Silva said he would be. We were forty miles plus when I saw my first glimpse of the long winged high flying frigate birds. With this sight all of my pain and anguish just seemed to vanish. I could now see what appeared to be two boats. I was getting closer to them, when out of nowhere I heard the roar of an airplane. De Silva was buzzing me as he said he would. He came so low and close that I could see him giving me thumbs up; he was waving and pointing for me to follow. My crew looked up and smiled. I heard Dirk say, "Nice one, Captain!"

Immediately Dirk and Bart went to work preparing tackle to begin our day of ahi fishing. De Silva was circling a spot near to where we were. Once there we put out the first lures. Before we could get them in the rigger both lines were solidly bit. We had been trolling less than a minute and already had a double hook up of large 200 pound plus ahi. The ahi were soon boated and placed in my brine box tuna coffin. Tachibana quit complaining and pointed the way to the airplane circling a spot off our port side. This was it; we were thick into the schooling ahi. The real challenge was my daily battle dealing with Mother Nature who was showing us no mercy; catching the ahi was merely a byproduct of the extreme difficulty we had to endure.

The fishing was great, the boating aspect pure hell. At the end of the first day my crew was beaten and exhausted. We were ahead in the point standing, but at what cost to the boat and crew? They said I looked different when I climbed down from the tower. I was not the man who had climbed up there only ten hours earlier. And to this day I admit that the man standing on the deck of *Black Bart* never again was the same. I had no strength left to help haul our tunas ashore or to help clean the boat and prepare it for the next day of competition. It took all the strength I had left just to climb up onto the dock and feel solid ground. It was only when I stood on that dock looking back into *Black Bart* that sanity returned to me. But the pain in my ribs returned along with my sanity. Whoever that man was who stood in the tower that day, it was not the same man who was now standing on the pier. While I remained business-like and professional in my approach to preparations for the following day's tournament quest, I was more like myself, and not the driven maniac who had inhabited the tower this day. I received some strange looks from Tachibana and the crew. They looked at me like they no longer knew me. But Tachibana would admit that he liked that character who was up there being tossed around in the tower.

That lunatic was going to win him the tournament and, to him, that was all that really mattered.

An inspection of my side revealed a horrific purple bruise to my rib cage. The pain remained with me; breathing was very difficult. (Later x-rays would reveal that one rib was fractured, several others were badly bruised). There was dread onboard *Black Bart* as the plan to return to the previous day's spot was made known. Tachibana knew and agreed, if we were to win this tournament, and there was never a doubt that we had the passion for this quest, then we had to go where the tuna were. And the tuna were not in the lee of the island, they were in the teeth of the maelstrom. Get ready men, we're going back!

I cinched my ribs up using duct tape. It was still very painful to touch that area and, aside from the fact that we might capsize and lose the boat and our lives, our next most serious concern was that I might be too incapacitated to perform in the tower. I prepared myself mentally for the challenge. There was no way I was going to give up.

Immediately upon stepping onto the deck of the Merritt, my mind took me to that place where it had gone the previous day. I was possessed, nearly insane, with the obsession to complete this job and to win this tournament. We would make it back out to the tuna grounds and we would fish all day, or we would die trying. Either result was perfectly all right with me.

The second day of fishing was a mirror of the first. Tachibana sent his Japanese crew but chose not to accompany us. However, the long-line boats and spotter plane were there each day with us as we struggled out to the same spot. The crew got sick, and my ribs were killing me from being tossed about. I kept telling myself, "It's mind over matter. I can do this." The boating conditions were awful again, but as bad as that was, the fishing was that much better. We caught tuna; nice, big, fat 200 pounders, morning, noon and afternoon. By the time we got the word to stop fishing, we were loaded up. This day I allowed the crew to drive us home in the following sea. I stayed below and rested my weary body and aching side, but I maintained my mental rigidity throughout it all. And then, when we were safely parked in our slip, I stepped ashore and again, as it had the day before, my sanity returned. My crew was looking at me in a most peculiar way. I think I scared them.

Days three and four were no different than days one and two. We fought heavy winds and seas each of these days and I continued to be slammed around in my rudimentary harness at the top of the tower. My crew was exhausted from four days of punishing conditions. I was beyond that, but I would never give in. I just wasn't built that way. I would pay the price, then finish the job. Making decisions like these is easy when you are doing what you believe in and love. And we continued to catch those furious, fiery bombs, and we continued to pull ahead in the point standings.

These conditions continued to exist for the entire tournament. On the fifth day Tachibana took his place in the cockpit. All boats lined up and followed me to the north shore. Only six of the fleet of one hundred managed the feat successfully. I had a one hour head start on the other boats and that was just enough time to catch three good size ahi. We caught three more after the other boats arrived. There was no need to continue fishing. My crew took over, allowing me to rest on the down hill ride home. Sleep and peace of mind came easily. Our swords were back in their sheaths. Our Samurai victory was complete.

This was then, and still is now, the greatest victory of my career. One hundred boats competed in this 1975 Hawaiian International Allison Yellow Fin Tuna competition. I won this tournament by a separation of over 2000 points between first and second place. But the victory was much more than prize money and a trophy. This was not merely the competition of *Black Bart* and its crew against the one hundred to one odds competition of the fleet.

This was a defining moment in the building of my character. This was a point from which I could never return. A new man, a bigger, tougher and wiser man climbed down from that tower on the last day of the Pokai Bay Tournament of 1975.

Each of the six man team received traditional fresh Plumeria flower leis. Each team member was smiling for the cameras while clutching and kissing their trophies. A winning celebration is always blessed as a memorable occasion. This victory win meant the most to me simply because of the tests and challenges I had to meet along the way from day one to day end. It is now thirty years later and my winning record score of 2975 points for that tuna tournament has never been equaled.

My fresh Plumeria lei has long since faded into dust. My beautiful tuna trophy has been misplaced or lost. All that is left for me is this story that I am now relating lest I forget that special place, eyes shut, time standing still, wind swept blue water, vivid memory of youth passionately in love with life at its very best.

Aloha,

Captain Bart Miller.

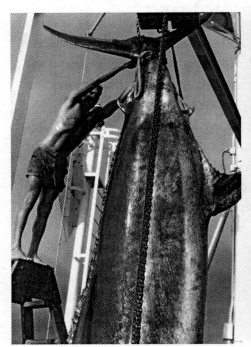

How big is a blue marlin that weights 1656 pounds? This big! This is the second largest blue marlin ever caught on rod and reel. March 16, 1984 on board *Black Bart* near the Otech Buoy off Kona Hawaii. Captain Bart Miller, angler Gary Merriman, mates Fran and Dominic, chartered by Rankin Smith, Jr. of Atlanta, GA.

The famous Merritt sport-fisherman *Black Bart* off the coast of Molokai
in the Hawaiian Islands-dressed out and ready for action

Captain
Peter Bristow

©Kevin Nakamaru

CAPTAIN PETER BRISTOW

I have often been asked where and when I started fishing. I never took the question seriously until Pat Mansell put it to me.

The first thing I can ever remember about fishing was during WW2. The place was the Bribie Passage off Caloundra near Brisbane, Australia. I was four years of age. We were in a rowing boat or punt. The water was so clear I could see right down to the bottom where the bream and flathead were swimming by. We were fishing while at anchor and, looking up, I remember those giant aircraft carriers and destroyers pass by almost over us as they entered Moreton Bay and the port of Brisbane. My Uncle Roy was a father figure to me in my fishing world. My real father was an engineer who sadly had no feeling for the sea.

Years later I was introduced to Point Lookout on Stradbroke Island. I joined a surf club and had a holiday there. It was at that time that I saw my first deep sea fishing from the deck of a dory that belonged to a local professional fisherman. That was a turning point in my life because I was so taken in by the ocean and the incredible fish I saw that nothing would ever be the same again.

For some years after this I spent competitive sailing with the Royal Queensland Yacht Club. This is incredibly good training for any young person. Not just in the way of boats but camaraderie and personal discipline. Also the respect of others who share the water with us.

For ten years I made my home at Point Lookout. I was fishing from the beach with nets and dories through the surf everyday.

I took three years, on and off with a prawn trawler up and down the coast. Best thing I ever did. There was only one boat I was on, the *Mororo II*. She was sixty-two feet and built and run by Don Mc Millan. He really was to me, the Old Man. The trawler fleet would wait outside the bar if things were bad to see if he would attempt a crossing. It was an experience that took exceptional skill and understanding. He passed on a great deal of knowledge to me.

About that time I saw an article in the Sunday Mail showing an American who was building a boat in Cairns to go look for Giant Black Marlin. I was taken in by the idea of this and it seemed to be a natural progression for me. By now I was running a charter boat in Moreton Bay and set my sights on Cairns. Some old pals from the Yacht Club and myself decided to give it a go for chartering a boat and fish for a week in Cairns. The year was 1968. That was the turning point in my life. No more prawn trawlers. No more commercial snapper fishing. It was marlin fishing from then on. I meet Peter Wright for the first time and made a life long friend of George Bransford. The friends I made in those early years in Cairns were the most wonderful group of people I have ever meet. It is hard to imagine how close the whole fleet of fishermen were. The anglers and crews and captains were the best in the world and we all had the greatest time in the greatest marlin fishery ever discovered.

I talked the owner of the charter boat into giving me a place as his crew for the following year. That went extremely well but there was no follow on as he sold the boat. There was nothing else to go on with and no other options so I decided to build the *Avalon*. That was 1969. I went down to Sydney and saw my old friend Bob Dyer. With his help the next season was fully booked for my boat before the keel had been laid. But I had no name for the boat. I was on a camping holiday down the coast with friends. About this time I was running out of cash and John Grey Gorton, Prime Minister of Australia had introduced the toughest credit restrictions since the Great Depression. I had to sell my two houses and property at Point Lookout in order to be able to carry on. My holiday friends said to me why don't you name the boat after the property at Point Lookout. So it was *Avalon*. That was a good name for a good boat.

One of the most satisfying periods of my time in the Cairns area was the formation of the Dunk Isle Classic. I am solely responsible for that. I got this off the ground with the help of a lot of friends and ran the tournament for many years.

I gave up on Cairns in 1991. With George Bransford and my wife, Pepe, as partners, I started a charter fishing business in Micronesia. Before long I had talked the local people and ex-patriot community into forming a fishing club. The Pohnpei Fishing Club is still going to this day. Elwood Harry gave us a good deal of help and we all had lots of fun with the proceedings.

Because of the economic climate in Japan at the time and the fervor pitch of fishing in Madeira it was an easy decision to make a move after five years. Besides, Pepe would be closer to her home in England. The *Katherine B* is still operating in Madeira.

There were various world and Australian Records on the way, but it is the fishing I remember, not the records.

ONLY ONE FISH
by
PETER BRISTOW

There was only one fish that ever impressed me. There was only one angler I ever thought of as the best. This is at the expense of so many fine anglers and good friends, but I am sure they would forgive me for thinking this way had they ever been privileged to be with this man on any day in his fishing life. In particular on that day when we saw that one fish.

He had many lives. Some dark and secretive, others flamboyant and outrageous. I brushed on some of them for moments of a glimpse into the depth of this man. Together with the greatest fish I have ever seen, his memory is indelible in my mind.

Jo Jo Del Guercio was born Elegio Del Guercio somewhere around 1932. He came from a background of wealth but was very quickly the black sheep of the family and liked to be on his own and doing his own thing. His mother was the first person to take him fishing somewhere down in the Florida Keys. He loved her very much for she shared this common interest and passion. The establishment never took him seriously for he had this rebel touch to his character that no one could relate to. He could be very outspoken to the point of embarrassment to sensitive people who did not understand. He would never tolerate incompetence and had a short fuse if he thought some blowhard was giving him a load of nonsense. He had an aura of power that was quite intimidating to many people. On the other hand, his heart could be so soft if he took a shine to someone.

But his strength and finesse with a rod and reel had to be seen to be believed. Over six years that covered twenty weeks of our time together on the reef, we developed a close relationship that is rare in any terms. We both had the team spirit. We both thought the same way about what we were doing and the respect was mutual. In addition to this I spent four seasons with him on his boat, the *No Problem,* on the rip off Bimini and Cat Cay. At the time of his death at the age of forty-six he was Commodore of Cat Cay Club in the Bahamas.

During those twenty weeks on the Great Barrier Reef, Jo Jo wrote in his diary that he had caught eighteen black marlin over one thousand pounds. We weighed only nine of those. The rest were tagged and released. Big fish were relatively common. Our estimates were always under. Well under.

Jo Jo had the ability to think like the fish. He could tell what they would do next and always knew where the fish was at any time. One day he said to me, "What do you think would happen if I went into free spool right after hook-up?"

My reaction was, "Well maybe the fish might do nothing at all." He agreed and we decided to try it out. The idea being that if the fish stayed still then we could creep up on it and pull a surprise tactic. This of course would only work on very big fish. The small ones seem to panic and break into a fast jumping run from the outset. The idea came from observations of big fish that some did nothing at all right after hook up.

I have heard the same comment about big blues but so far have not had the experience myself. These big blacks just swim along close to the surface. I assume they are trying to figure out what on earth is going on. So we tried the experiment with outstanding results. It seemed to work better with a small bait such as a scad. The strike drag was set at forty-five pounds with no drop back from the outrigger. When I called "big fish" Jo Jo took the strike from the rod holder in the covering board. After setting the hook he then threw the reel immediately into free spool and went to the chair. It did not seem to matter where Jo Jo was or what he was doing, by the time the line was tight on the rod tip he was there with the reel. He usually gave the fish some drop back but this depended on what kind of run off or pick up he was getting. His hookup rate was phenomenal. He hooked almost everything that looked at a bait.

Anyway, right after the strike and a short burst of the engines, I would slow down and that was the free spool point. After he literally jumped into the chair I would go into reverse with the boat. With just enough drag to pick up the line, Jo Jo would wind very slowly. The line was running loose straight down from the tip into the water and then across the surface to the fish. He would start to giggle, like the cackle of a small child eyeing off sweets in a candy store. He would look up at me with the most supercilious grin. We all knew what was going to happen. The reaction of the crew was close to shock horror. I always got roughly the same comment. "What the bloody hell do you want me to do with this ?" We had thirty foot double and thirty foot wire leader in those days. That meant with three turns of double on the reel, the fish was only fifty-five feet away or even less. Sometimes it was almost possible to have the snap right to the rod tip. That's only thirty feet. At that point I had to stop the boat. Then he would slam the drag all the way down. With a Fin-Nor on forty-five pound at a half, there was seventy-five in the corner. It was at this point that Jo Jo was standing on the fish with all his weight and hanging on to the chair as well with his right arm. This was enough to get the attention of the fish and give it the message that all was not well. The fish would then assume an angle to the surface and the bill would begin to swing from side-to-side. After a few seconds of this the power was transmitted to the tail and the weight of the fish was propelled forward and upward. What a spectacle. Enough to run a cold shiver down the spine of any wireman. Of course it might be an hour before we got that close to the fish again but that special moment of contact was with us forever.

Jo Jo was always trying to improve the game. He desperately tried to buy the Fin-Nor Reel company from Henry Bryer so that he could improve the product. There were so many annoying simple things that could be dealt with by someone who was so in tune with the industry. He invented the rocket launcher out of frustration while catching sailfish off Florida. To be able to stand in one place and hook up four fish without running around the cockpit made common sense to him.

To my knowledge he was the first person to put reinforcement into a seat harness. Alan Merritt did this for him by inserting an aluminum plate into the backing. I spoke at length to Jo Jo about building a fully fiberglass molded seat. Some years later after his death I completed the task and it made the finest harness I have ever seen.

His ability to fish the 130 tackle right to the limit and not break line was incredible. I only saw him break line twice. The first time was the fault of the old Fin-Nor guide. The back guide had the rollers on top of each other, in line. Out of frustration I spoke to Jack Erskin and by then Jo Jo had a share in Jack's tackle business. Jack got with Fin-Nor and they decided to make us a new guide with staggered rollers. They were the first heavy guides of this design. A few months later I was in the factory and took delivery of the first six sets back to Australia as a trial. Jack fitted them to the old Shakespeare "stump-pullers". The rods needed total rebuild as the number four guide had to be eliminated and the new rear guide moved forward.

The 12/0 Fin-Nor reel was still the only reel that was fishable. It was still the only reel on the market with a successful two speed gear box. We all used the same reel. All Dacron or Du Pont polyester was made by Western Filament and marketed by Garcia. It had a nick name amongst the fishing crews as "no breakum". It never let me down once.

The only other time I broke line with Jo Jo was when I ran over a small fish that had doubled back on me but the line did not break at that point. I dived over the side and lifted the line off the rudder. We got the fish near the boat and put some extra pressure on when the line went pop. In fact that was the day Jo Jo caught the most giant blacks caught by any angler in one day. This was not the day of the one big fish but I should put it down now just for the record.

I have told the story many times to many unbelievers. We had the mother ship *Tropic Queen* parked at the bottom of Number Ten Ribbon Reef. On board was Jo Jo, Capt. Bill Staros, mates Gordon Hallam and George York and myself. We had been traveling north from Cairns for about a week. Slowly working our way from one anchorage to the next, catching marlin all the way and building up a good supply of bait. The date was October 8, 1973.

That morning is as vivid in my mind as if it was happening today. I ran out of the anchorage at 9:00 AM around the southern tip of the reef and along the back of the surf to keep away from the choppy water. It was blowing fifteen to twenty knots SE trade wind. There was a good current running south against the trade making for a good sea on the drop-off. As the reef started to swing to the north I headed out to where I would pick up the drop. This happened around the fifty fathom line and I eased back on the throttles.

I glanced back at the *Tropic Queen* and was comfortable with the angle I had with the anchorage. Then I set the throttles to the correct trolling speed. Not until then did l look back behind the *Avalon*. What meet my eyes was a sight that all fishermen only dream about but rarely ever see. At that point there were between forty and fifty giant blacks behind the boat. There were about ten fish at the transom trying to eat the paint work. Each wave in succession looking back had about another ten fish in it. The sight was unbelievable and defies words to describe. The color was intense. The fish being all together and competing for attention were lit up like balls of blue fire. The ones right behind the transom were dark brown in body with bright blue pecs. The ones further back tended to be more blue all over.

The air was screaming with shouting from the most excited group of fishermen I can remember. "Get em out, get em out ," is all I can remember saying myself. It was impossible to get two baits in the water. We put one rig inside and Jo Jo stayed in the chair and would free spool as far as he thought was needed. All that was necessary was to just hold the spool then let it go after the strike. That took only and a few seconds of trolling. The hook was set at forty-five pounds and in no time another fish was tagged and released.

We caught eleven fish straight, all tagged and released. The fish went off the bite for a while after that. They were just picking at the bait. We were pulling hooks or getting foul hooked. This is often what puts a lot of fishermen on the wrong track. Don't change tack was our motto. When they are ready they will bite properly. I can't remember what time it was exactly but early afternoon they turned it on again. The first good hook up was a nice fish and we decided to put it in the boat. It went 1,127 on the scales that evening. The bite was not as hot as in the morning and we were by now able to put two rods out. After boating that fish around 2:00 PM we caught nine straight. Gordon was suffering the stretch arm syndrome so Yorky stepped in to help out. George was a very strong fellow and did not like to let go the wire. Consequently three were broken off at the boat. Jo Jo's reaction was that he really didn't care about the tag that much and he was going to count the fish as caught anyway. I agree. We fished until late and Gordon had long run out of rigged bait.

Jo Jo called for the bait to be rigged by just passing the hook through the eyes. He would free spool to the peg marker and the scad would pop up and flip over a few times. That's all it took to get a bite. In all we had thirty fish on and caught twenty. That included the one in the boat and sixteen tags.

The last strike was at 7:00 PM at the bottom of Number Ten Ribbon. It was dark but the moon was right on full with a high tide about 7:30. The tide was flooding up through the opening between Nine and Ten, which made the water flat and glassy. I could not see the opening. I could see absolutely nothing except the lights of the *Tropic Queen* and the after glow of the sunset. This glow and the light of the full moon made for zero visibility of the coral reefs and bommies that choked the entrance. Apart from staying outside the reef all night there was only one thing for it. I had all on board go stand up on the bow to counter the weight of the fish in the pit. With all the old Perkins could give me, I ran right across the bottom of Number Ten Ribbon. There were some interesting comments coming from the bow of the *Avalon* as the coral flashed by underneath.

Full moon meant the tide was a good one and I calculated about nine feet of water but took the risk of hitting one of the loose stones that sit up on the top of the reef. I have thought about it since and get a strange feeling in my gut.

It all went well. It was the best days fishing we ever had. What made it possible was the undying strength of Jo Jo. I notice that when he became a little tired he would take deep breathing for a few moments. He never let himself get to the point of full exhaustion. We were all exhausted and were in bed by 8:30.

Next morning as we were leaving the mother ship, Jo Jo handed me a pair of deck shoes. I said, "What's this for ?"

He said, "That's just in case we have to walk home this evening!" (Number Ten Ribbon is twenty-five miles offshore).

The fish went off the bite a bit the next day and we had sixteen bites and caught only eight up to 950 pounds. They were hot in the morning but tapered off in the afternoons. The next day was quiet. Only two fish, 800 and 950. The fish were still there but only picking. The sea was flat and we were blaming the calm weather It was not until the third day that I was able to turn the radio back on. There had been no time for the usual chit chat that goes on. It was an old AM set or double side band in those days. No sooner had I switched it on than Peter Wright called me up and wanted to know where I was and what I was doing. I apologized for the radio silence and gave him a brief summary of events over the past few days. There was silence. He did not answer back in his usual fashion. I called him up and said, "Are you still there Peter ?"

There was a pause and he came back with, "Yes, but I am being sick."

I must admit it was overwhelming even for the most seasoned veterans of the sea. For the three week trip Jo Jo caught ninety-six fish. That was 1973, and it was the best year I ever had.

We never saw the repeat of that first encounter ever again. It only happened the once on the first time we raised the fish. I have never seen it before or since. It was truly the most amazing sight. The sight of a life time.

* * * * * * * * * * * * * * *

Before I get to the story about the Big Fish I think there are a few points worth discussing about these big fish. Foremost on my mind is the aspect of their vulnerability to capture. There are, in my opinion, three main places in time when this might take place. Let us assume that we are talking about 1,000 pounds and upwards. Right after hook-up there is a brief period when sometimes the fish will do nothing at all. This time relates to the first few paragraphs in this story and can be a very serious time for making quick decisions to cut the fish free or to stroke the gaff. This can only be achieved by the most competent crew. There is no room for error.

Then there is a period that is reached after a good series of jumping runs when the fish has run out of puff but is not completely exhausted. This can be about fifteen or twenty minutes after hook-up. If the fish shows itself and boat handling can put the crew right on top of the fish, all can go well with good results. That is the point where Jo Jo would cut the wire should the occasion arise.

The final stage is when the fish is completely exhausted. If all goes well, a good angler is going to whip a healthy fish into submission in about one to one and a half hours on 130 pound tackle, that is if the fish does some jumping and is not hooked in the corner of the jaw. This can extend the fight for it may not be possible to land the fish.

A good example of the twenty minute period came one day in the early 70's. We had the mother ship at No Name Reef just north of Number Ten. It had been a good day with quite a few big fish. Late afternoon I was heading north toward the opening at the top of Ten. Somewhere about Heartbreak Corner we were surfing down some very large sea. The late afternoon sun was driving deep into the face of the sea and from the back of the wave I could see this great fish coming through. It tracked down the face of the wave and got sight of the scad. It bolted out of the water and attacked the scad from an airborne position. It completely missed the bait and skittered around still out of the water and took it going back the other way. My first estimate was 1,100. We had the fish to the boat in about twenty minutes. Great jumping, great angling, and great team work. There was a big sea running, but then it all went wrong. There was some confusion at the back of the boat and the tag did not go in. Right then Sam Leiser let the wire go.

Jo Jo blew up. "What the hell is going on? Now I have to catch this thing again."

The fish went down and was very hard to control in the big sea. It regained its strength and settled down to fight the good fight.

It took one and a half hours to get that fish along side again. It was a beast. From that point onward, Jo Jo kept a pair of wire cutters on the footrest. When the mate took the leader Jo Jo would drop one foot to the floor, reach forward and grab hold of the wire and cut. His policy was that if the tag did not go in, that was too bad. Why fight a fish to exhaustion just for the sake of a tag. Never mind wearing the angler out in the process. I made that standard policy from then on.

* * * * * * * * * * * * * * * * *

There was one other fish for Jo Jo that sticks in my mind and illustrates how hard a fish can pull when it does nothing and is hooked in the corner of the jaw. The date was October 10, 1972. It was late afternoon, flat calm off Anderson Reef. Bill Staros was sitting on the bridge with me. He was telling me stories of Bimini and how some old fisherman there would go offshore late in the afternoon. Apparently he would quite often catch a big blue on this tack. I decided to give it a go.

I must have gone off the edge about five or six miles. The reef was out of sight and I could not see the *Tropic Queen* anchored behind North Escape. I was making a turn to head back. Half way through the turn this creature climbed all over the bonito that was skipping along on the left rigger. That's all we saw. The great head and bill, and then a tail as it disappeared into the depths. Long runs, then the steady track off shore. Without any doubt or exception these big fish head exactly east on the compass. It would be possible to make a compass adjustment was there any doubt about the heading. It is always absolutely east, directly away from the reef.

This fish actually changed the opinion that Jo Jo had for the giant black. Until then he was of the firm belief that the black marlin was not to be taken seriously. They were just big, that's all! Bill

Carpenter described them as pussy cats, and who was there to disagree with him? He had been down to Cabo Blanco and tangled with a few fish. I don't know how many or when. I was talking to him at Cat Cay in the early 70's and asked him when he would fish the reef. He was, in his day, the foremost tuna fisherman who had ever gone down the rip looking for bluefin. He was well known as Mr. Tuna. He told me that the blacks had never impressed him but I had trouble understanding why. At the time we spoke, he was having trouble with his hips which eventually turned out to be cancer and was to take his life. But his legacy of the blacks left everyone guessing as to their prowess as a fighter.

This fish turned the tide in Jo Jo's mind. It was the longest he was to ever spend on any fish he was to fight in his career. He was over two hours getting the fish to the double, then another forty-five minutes before we could use a gaff. With the Fin-Nor wound up all the way on the vernier there was 110 pounds in the corner. It stayed that way for twenty minutes with Jo Jo holding the spool as well as the chair to stop the run off. Then Sam got the wire and that went on for another twenty minutes. By the time it was over both men were exhausted. Jo Jo confided with me later that he had what he thought only another ten minutes left in him. The fish was hooked in the corner of the jaw and had brought both men to their knees. With today's popular use of the circle hook it gives an interesting aspect to that style of fishing. It will make the fish far more difficult to catch in general and increase the risk of shark problems.

An interesting note here. The fish went 1,211 pounds. That evening at the back of our mother ship, Pat Gay and Dennis Wallace(Brazzaka) came over for a drink and to see the fish. Pat Gay said to me it was the biggest marlin he had seen to that date. Brazzaka came on board the *Avalon* to see the tackle after hearing the stories about the excessive drag that Jo Jo was capable of. He put on a glove and took a couple of wraps. He lifted his leg and put his foot on the reel. As hard as he could pull he was not able to move the spool!

We went fishing for another week without as much as getting a strike. I fished south all the way to Jenny Louise Shoal and had one more bite. The fish weighed 1,200. Two 1,200 pounders back-to-back but seven days apart. Slow fishing. Ha!

* * * * * * * * * * * * * * *

Now I come to the "one fish" that we came in contact with in 1975. It had been a good season. We had our share of big fish. That year I had managed to get both Jo Jo and Bill Staros into the water for a swim on the reef. That in itself was an accomplishment. Bill rarely or never went swimming. He was very self-conscious of his skinny legs and earned the name of "Sparrow Legs" as a result. His brother George never gave up on teasing him. No wonder he never wanted to swim. Poor chap was so embarrassed, he never wore shorts.

The swimming was something that I strongly promoted to everyone as purely a good form of exercise. Although it can be very tiring on board ship for weeks on end, there is little form of exercise. What better way to indulge than to snorkel and free dive for an hour each morning on the most beautiful coral reef in the world?

But it did not wash with Jo Jo. Although he was quite happy to see us all go in for a swim, he was quite happy to read a book, but not for long. The fishing always had priority. I often saw that look of impatience when my crew were still in the water soaking up the ambience of the Great Barrier Reef.

Late one afternoon we were working our way south towards Cairns. It had been a two week trip north to Number Ten and this evening I had the *Tropic Queen* anchored at North Escape. I passed Anderson Reef and was turning in toward Escape. The light was bright but the sun was low making the water dark. I had a bonito skipping off the left rigger and a scad on the right. I always fished the same way so as to reduce confusion at the time of a strike. When I called left rigger, everyone knew it was a big bait and dealt with the drop back accordingly.

What took place in the matter of a few minutes is an event, the memory of which I will take to my grave. Jo Jo sat cross legged on the starboard bunk most of the time smoking cigarettes and reading some book or the other. He did not seem to have any preference in literature. It had been a quiet day but the wind was up and there was no warning of the strike. The fish came from left to right on the left rigger. There was a bonito of the Kawa-Kawa variety. We called them mackerel tuna. It was rigged with a single hook, a Mustad 7690, size 16/0 on the top of the head. The leader was .040 galvanized single strand wire that broke around 550 pounds.

My first impression was that a good sized wahoo was jumping over the bait. Things happen quickly, but in the flash of time, the human brain is able to make decisions and often makes mistakes. The huge head and dorsal fin was three feet high. It was many times bigger than anything I had ever seen. Then the enormous tail went over in an arc like a giant saber. It seemed to be eighteen feet behind the head. There was a slow pick up and after what seemed an eternity, Jo Jo put the drag onto strike. I gave the boat the usual spurt to come tight and to be going ahead should the fish decide to jump toward us, in which case I would be going in the right direction. Nothing happened. The fish moved slowly but deliberately in an easterly direction. I was too shaken by the size of the fish to say much. I know I did say one thing, "Put the gaffs down."

On board was Jo Jo, Capt. Bill Staros, Sam Leiser, Jo Jo's wireman from Florida, and my crew, Trevor Wilkinson and me.

Most of us had seen many big fish before this, but no one was ready for this. It seemed like only a few minutes and the fish was close. Next thing Sam had the wire. Only fifteen minutes had elapsed.

Jo Jo looked up at me and said, "What are you going to do Peter?"

I remember saying, "What do you think?"

"We have to take our shot," he said. "Let's have a go."

Then the fish jumped on the wire. First of all the head came outside on to us and stayed there. Then slowly two thirds of the body rose out of the water. It just hung there motionless. Then it slid back slowly until only the bill was showing. Once again it repeated this action exactly as before. If that was not enough, it did the exact same thing again. Sam had at least ten feet of wire behind him, but no one was going to cut it on this occasion. Being so close for so long and side on to us, it was possible to make a very good size assessment. With the body of the fish two thirds out of the water, I was looking directly into the eye of this giant. I estimate the total length to be about eighteen feet. With my arms outstretched I would have just been able to wrap half the girth. I was shaking.

Then the fish laid down and was swimming slowly at the corner of the transom. Trevor went for the gaff and got a good shot in the shoulder. Right at this point the wire broke. I don't know why. Sam stood there looking at the broken end in his hand. Bill was standing behind Sam with the other gaff and had become mesmerized by all that was happening. I was screaming by this point for the other gaff but it was too late. The wire is as good as a gaff and now broken the fish suddenly took off before Trevor got to the cleat. So now it was a crisis. The only contact we had with the fish was one gaff in the back. I was praying for the fish to come to the surface and show itself again but not so. It took off to the east steadily gathering speed. We were doing five or six knots. We started taking green water over the stern. It was turning the cockpit into a swimming pool. The gaff rope was like a steel rod. The fish had the boat down by the stern and was in process of taking us down with it. The carpet inside between the bunks was washed down forward. We were sinking with the fish.

I wanted to go ahead and stop all this but was hoping and praying that the fish would give up and come back to the surface. It never happened. When it finally seemed that disaster was close, the gaff pulled out. No one could speak. I put the boat in gear and headed slowly for the anchorage. Back onboard we sat there looking at each other trying to come to terms with the events of the past hour. There was no witch hunt, no one was to blame. But I have always held myself accountable for the cock-up. That was our fish, but we messed up. I did.

Jo Jo had resigned himself to losing the fish. He never carried a grudge. We always spoke about events as they happened and were always open about what went wrong. This is the only way to deal with the situation. With this attitude it is possible to face the next day with a fresh spirit. His opinion was that we had to take that shot when we did or we may never have seen that fish again. I believe that.

One thing Jo Jo said to me was like he was reading my mail. He said, "Do you know what ran through my mind when that fish hit? I thought a forty-five pound wahoo was jumping over the bonito." I looked at him in disbelief. That's exactly what I was thinking.

Jo Jo was always very good on estimates and meticulous on the figures. With the estimated measurements we came to a minimum weight of 2,100 pounds. That was running the formula without adding the ten percent allowable for billfish should they carry an anal girth equal to or greater than the girth at the shoulder. One can add this percentage with discretion. An educated guess can be very accurate, considering the figures already given. He later put it in print that he thought the fish was 1,800. I think he was being modest and kind to the skeptics. After all it seems outrageous that anyone should claim to have had a fish so big. After all, it was only one fish.

SOME OTHER FISH OF INTEREST WITH JO JO

ALMOST IN THE BOAT

There was one year when George Staros was onboard as well. So we had Bill and George known to all of us as the "Greeks". They were a formidable pair in the tournament scene. With Jo Jo they won the Bimini and Cat Cay tournaments year after year. Jo Jo twice won the coveted Masters at the Sailfish Club of Palm Beach, a feat not repeated since by any other angler.

Also, my crew then was Mike Banham, nicknamed the Kona Kid by Lee Marvin. Mike was a great crewman but had a bad habit of trying to hang on to the wire for too long. A few days before, his hand had been badly crushed by the wire and put him out of action, a direct result of hanging on for too long. He did this once too often in Hawaii and was dragged over the stern by a green fish. Bobby Brown almost ran over him while backing down, but got lucky to find Mike pop up under the bow of the boat covered with bottom paint. A narrow escape.

We had been up north on a long mothership trip and were working our way south for our last days fishing off Lyndon Bank before running into Cairns. It was flat calm. The Bank looked like a mackerel fleet had moved in with all the boats there. I was cruising down through the fleet when around the top of the bank this huge fish climbed onto a bonito skipping off the left rigger. Within ten minutes and without any jumping the fish was swimming close by and along with us on the left side. It was totally disoriented and did not seem to know what was going on. From the bridge I called 1,100. We all agreed that the fish would be released.

Now George Staros had developed a serious problem with his back. He had a nerve being pinched off between two vertebrae and was in severe pain and without medication. Withstanding all this he was still managing to help out when necessary. So this left only Bill and myself to assist Jo Jo with the wire and driving the boat. I elected to wire the fish and Bill came up on the bridge to drive. I got hold of the wire and the next thing that happened, the fish decided to jump. Not away, as usual but straight at me. I don't think Bill could have done anything on the wheel as it all happened too quickly. The fish was balancing on the covering board with the bill hanging down behind the chair. We almost had 1,100 pounds of brand new marlin in the boat with us. It flicked its head up in a stiffening manner and I was able to get my shoulder under the head. But the tail could still hit the water and propel it forward.

In a joking manner I called out to Mike, "Tag the bloody thing." I looked around to see him and George huddled up near the ice box at the forward end of the cabin. Profound bad language was all I got which translated into, "Get rid of the thing." They wanted no part of it.

By this time Jo Jo had unharnessed himself and was ready to abandon me and the cockpit. "The wire's cut, he's all yours," I heard him say. I don't know how long it took. Not long, but it slid back into the water. Then it made another rush at us and punched a good sized hole in the side of the *Avalon.* We plugged the hole with a large Coke bottle wrapped with a piece of cloth. It remained there until I made up a large wooden plug. I carried a selection of tapered plugs for this kind of thing but nothing so large.

* * * * * * * * * * * *

ANOTHER CLOSE CALL

The last year that Jo Jo fished the GBR was 1977. He meet his untimely death in February the following year. He had put his weight back on and was back to his usual strength and fighting fit. The year before he had turned up in Cairns only a shadow of his former self. He had been on this ridiculous Dr. Atkins diet. It absolutely sapped him of his strength. He was exhausted after every fish. He frightened me. First up, I thought he had the big "C" until he told me about the diet. He looked horrible. He told me he would quit the diet when he got home and he did.

We did not break any records that year but had the most phenomenal run of big fish I have ever seen. We only put four of them in the boat, the biggest 1,325 and the smallest 1,175. There was a body of fish off Number Four Ribbon. In three days we caught thirty fish, the smallest being around 700. We were releasing thousand pound fish one after another. Very few of them were tagged. Bill Staros had the idea that the tags were helping the long-liners. I strongly disagreed with him and we had some words, but that was it. Why make a fuss. We were out there to have fun. I always tried to avoid any confrontation. Right to this day I still believe in tagging every fish released.

Brian Reeves was on the deck and we had some help from a couple of young American crew who were along for the ride. It was blowing a stiff SE trade and the sea was standing up pretty good on the outside corner of Number Four. This was right where the South Equatorial Current was pushing south and hard against the breeze. This was right where the fish were. I would hook up and fight the fish. Then the release would usually take place north of the hookup point. The fish tend to run with the sea right after being hooked. After releasing the fish I would run up sea, back to the spot before putting a bait in the water.

On one occasion a fish about 850 pounds hooked up and took off up-sea into the wind. Most unusual. The fish took off on its first sizzling run, but not for long. I just sat there waiting for something to happen. No use going anywhere until the fish decided which way to go. The sea was extra big and the *Avalon* was laying beam-to in the trough. The fish made its first jump on the top of this huge wave that was coming right for me. I was looking right up at it. Then it went into the water and came out immediately, but heading right at us--amidships. It had the added momentum of the face of the sea like a dolphin does riding a wave. I was dead in the water and still in the trough. I slammed both engines forward and gave every bit of power I could find. Thank God there was no delay in the gear boxes or this story would have a different ending. The boys were getting the other rod out of the way and maybe reaching for a camera. There was no one else in the cockpit but Jo Jo who was in the chair by this time. His immediate reaction was to wind like a machine and take up the slack as the fish rushed at him. A good angler? The best!

The next jump was half way down the face of the sea still heading at us about the forward end of the cockpit. In the split seconds of time it took, I recall looking into the pit and screaming, "Watch out!" By now the boat had moved forward a few feet, but not nearly enough for comfort. Jo Jo dropped one foot to the floor and ducked. He had wound the line in almost to the snap. The fish cleared the transom by about five feet, not behind the stern, but over it. The little bit of slack caught up with the rod tip as the fish went past and it was the closest thing to whiplash I have ever seen. The chair spun around at the same speed the fish was traveling. Just remember, he still had forty-five pounds of strike drag on the Fin-Nor. Thank God it did not take a turn around the rod tip. I doubt it would have jerked him out of the boat. The fish was going too fast and the inertia of his heavy body would have been hard to move. It would have just broken the line or the wire. Had I not moved the boat at all, the fish would have gone in one side of the cabin and out the other. I have no doubt about that. Anyone in its way would have perished.

There is one very important message here for any angler. When there is loose wire near the rod tip from behind a mate taking the leader, or in the situation just described, it is imperative for the rod tip to be as low as possible to horizontal. This could save your life.

I can't remember any more about that fish. I think the shock might have blanked out my memory.

The world famous angler JoJo DelGuercio on the docks in Bimini, Bahamas with two giant blue fin tuna. JoJo gained a reputation in his time as perhaps the greatest angler of large pelagic species in the world.

"Brazakka"
Captain Dennis Wallace

©Kevin Nakamaru

CAPTAIN DENNIS 'BRAZAKKA' WALLACE

THE MAN BEHIND THE LEGEND

We can only ponder at what went through George Bransford's mind who, as a young American paratrooper based in northern Queensland during WWII looked down upon the cobalt waters of the Coral Sea beyond the Great Barrier Reef east of Cairns in northeastern Australia. What we do know for sure is that when he was in Cairns, Bransford, who ran a small charter boat operation back home at Fort Lauderdale in Florida, talked to the local mackerel fishermen who told him tales of huge sea creatures stealing their fish and smashing their gear.

Having caught small blue marlin, sailfish, tuna, mackerel and dolphin fish back home, Bransford imagined that the thieves were blue marlin and sailfish, and that the sizes of some of them described by the disgruntled fishermen were gross exaggerations - as is the way of men of the sea. Nothing could be that big. Never in his wildest dreams could George Bransford have imagined what huge critters lived beyond the outer Great Barrier Reef. But he could see that there was an opportunity there for an enterprising young fellow, so in the early 1960's he returned to Cairns with his wife and family to live. He had a wooden twenty-nine foot single diesel engined game boat built, named it *Sea Baby* and hung his shingle out on the wharf to take tourists big game fishing.

But in those days Cairns, a town that survived solely on the back of sugar cane and beef cattle, was hardly a tourist destination. Business wasn't good. And little wonder. To get to the outer reef, Bransford had to day-trip the thirty odd miles at an agonizingly slow ten to twelve knots, punching into a southeast trade wind most of the way. In fact business was so bad that Bransford had to explore the waters beyond the Great Barrier Reef using his deckhand, Richard Obach, as the angler. Obach, a twenty-four year old New Yorker who was traveling around Australia on an adventure holiday, had never rigged a bait in his life before he met Bransford. But he was in for the adventure of a lifetime. Bransford would tell his deckie time and again that 'all he needed was that one big fish' to make his belief in Cairns come true. And soon enough his patience paid off.

On 10 September, 1966, using a black-faced Penn Senator filled with eighty pound monofilament line and a gamefishing rod with no roller guides, Obach lost a fish after a five hour battle that was later estimated at between 1,500 and 2,000 pounds. On 24 September they landed a 1,064 pound black marlin that was not only the new world record for a black on eighty pound tackle, but the first 1,000 pound plus marlin ever landed anywhere in the world on eighty pound gear.

In a heartbeat Cairns became the black marlin capital of the world and in the years to come prospered beyond anyone's wildest imagination. Since that wonderful day in 1966 hundreds of thousand pound black marlin - the biggest 1,442 pounds - have been weighed and many, many more tagged and released.

And with it's new found notoriety Cairns spawned the greatest fleet of game fishing boats and colourful characters the world of big black marlin fishing has ever seen. And none of those characters are more colourful than Captain Dennis 'Brazakka' Wallace.

Legend has it that as a baby, little Dennis fell from the back of a truck in the Australian desert and was found and raised by a nomadic tribe of Aboriginals who named him 'Brazakka' which, in their ancient dialect, means 'wild man'. Fact or fiction, the legend has stuck.

Brazakka went to sea at fifteen working the back-breaking trawlers off Evans Head on the northern New South Wales coast, and at eighteen he had chalked up enough sea hours to gain his Masters ticket and become one of the youngest skippers on the eastern seaboard. The following seven years he worked the prawn trawlers from southern Queensland all the way around the top and down into the Gulf of Carpentaria until he had enough to get his own boat.

When Richard Obach caught his big fish in 1966, word spread like a bushfire fanned by gale force winds. Far away in the Gulf, Brazakka heard the story and wanted to become a part of the fledgling game fishing industry. One day perhaps. For now he had a young family to feed and trawler to pay off.

The following year Alan Collis with his locally built *Marlan* made the gamefishing fleet two. Brazakka knew what he wanted to do and the following season he took the biggest punt of his life. He sold his prawn trawler and took his family to Cairns. By this time George Bransford had built the *Sea Baby II* and, knowing little about big game fishing but with more than enough knowledge of boats and the sea to get him by, Brazakka bought the tiny *Sea Baby* and became the third charter operator in the Cairns game fishing fleet.

But with the opposition now in faster boats and not enough customers to go around, and even though he caught some respectable fish in his first season, including a thousand pounder, Brazakka went broke and had to sell his little boat. It taught him a bitter lesson. From then on he adopted (for boats) his oft-quoted philosophy; "If it flies, floats or fucks - rent it."

From 1970 until 1975 Brazakka leased a variety of privately owned game boats on a profit share basis with their owners for the season from late August through to December. This way he earned much more than he would by owning the boat and he had none of the worries. During that time he weighed eighteen black marlin over a grand including one of 1,320 pounds.

As Brazakka's reputation as a fisherman and a charismatic character grew, so did his clientele from all over the world. One of them was Dick Schubert, a mega-rich American who, among a multitude of other investments, owned seventeen MacDonald's franchises throughout the States. Brazakka and Schubert went into business together. Brazakka designed a boat and Schubert gave him an open cheque to build it.

But it was no ordinary boat. Brazakka had long seen the potential of taking as many as four anglers to sea for a seven, ten or fourteen day charter (or sometimes longer) on a fully self-contained live-aboard game fishing boat, instead of having to either day trip each day out of Cairns and return at night or charter a mother ship at exorbitant cost.

Sea Venture was the first of her kind. Built by Frank Woodnutt in Cairns - who by now had become the most famous boat builder in the country and had built about half of the now burgeoning Cairns fleet - she was fifty-four feet in length with a tower, had every modern convenience for the era, a desalinater so they never ran out of fresh water, double the refrigeration storage space of any other boat, and was powered by twin V8 871 GM diesels that pushed her along at up to twenty-five knots.

Sea Venture had accommodation for four anglers, the captain, cook and two crew, and the range to fish north to as far as Lizard Island trolling the Ribbon Reefs along the way. And when it was time for the anglers to go home, a float plane would arrive from Cairns with the next charter and more supplies, and take the departing charter back. *Sea Venture* fueled up from the mother ships at sea and could stay out the whole season without having to go back to port. It was a better deal all round for everyone. 'Build her and they will come'. And they did. In their droves. Brazakka had a full book every year. And just so that everyone knew who she was, Brazakka had *Sea Venture* painted bright yellow.

And so the legend of the wild man in his yellow boat grew. Brazakka became a celebrity in his own right, featured in beer commercials, the movie *Brazakka's Reef* with Lee Marvin, a profile of his life on Australian *60 Minutes*, articles about him in fishing magazines in Australia and around the world, and a bit part in a Lee Marvin Hollywood movie. In more recent years he was a regular on Steve Irwin's *Crocodile Man* series. Big game fishing had it's own superstar.

And, as befitting gamefishing royalty, his clientele read like a Who's Who. Author Wilbur Smith, Ernest Borgnine and ex-President Jimmy Carter to name a few. Brazakka also became the Australian captain to one of America's most colourful characters, multi-billionaire Arkansas farmer Don 'Chickenman' Tyson who supplies twenty-five percent of America with its chickens. A founding member of the Billfish Foundation, Tyson was the International Gamefishing Association Trustee and is a member of the IGFA Hall of Fame.

But without doubt his most famous client was American actor Lee Marvin who, in twelve seasons fishing with Brazakka, weighed thirteen granders and tagged at least a dozen more that would have made it. One of Marvin's fish - taken on his first charter with Brazakka in 1973 - was 1,320 pounds. Little wonder he kept coming back.

Now 60, Brazakka lives on his ranch in the lush rainforest district high on the Atherton Tablelands overlooking Cairns. He doesn't fish the season full time anymore, choosing rather to take private charters on their boats for a couple of weeks should the occasion arise.

Ever the adventurer, these days Brazakka operates his fleet of six commercial helicopters and personally specialises in taking anglers and hunters in his chopper 'heli-fishing' deep into far north Queensland to catch barramundi in estuaries and land-locked lagoons and shoot feral pigs on the savannas.

Here are just a couple of the many stories from Brazakka's lifetime of adventures at sea ...

LEE'S LAST FISH
by
BRAZAKKA

I first met Lee Marvin in a bar in Kona in early 1973. After we got to talking a while I discovered that even though he had never been there he knew more about Cairns and the fishing than most of the locals. We put a charter together for November and it was the beginning of a life-long friendship. As it turned out the 1973 season was a ball-tearer. In ten day's fishing Lee and his party weighed four fish over a grand - three for Lee including a monster of 1,320 pounds - and a 1,030 pounder for his wife, Pam. The craggy-faced ex-marine turned superstar who had seen eyeball-to-eyeball action in the Pacific during World War II, was hooked. This would be just the first of many visits.

Any special memories? Millions of 'em. But there is one thousand pounder that will stay with me forever for a very special reason . . .

Lee stole another foot of line with one crank of the 12/0 Fin Nor's handle. The black marlin he had hooked had sounded itself into the bottomless pit off the continental shelf. The fish had tailed the skipping tuna bait for about ten minutes before wolfing it down like a rhino eats a peanut. One spectacular leap on hook-up let me know it was big. But just how big?

"She's big and fat. I think she's a horse, Lee," I called to my angler from the tuna tower. That was an hour ago. Now every bone in Lee's body was grizzling as he fought for every inch of line.

"Why do I keep doing this to myself, Mate?" he called back. "Haven't I had enough granders?"

He knew very well he hadn't. He was a marlin junkie and the uncertainty of each fish was his fix. No two were ever the same. Some became confused and thrashed around on the surface to be gaffed or tagged in a few minutes. Others sounded and died on you after fifteen hours in the chair.

This fish had peeled off 300 yards of 130 pound line on its first grey-hounding run like it was toilet paper off a roll. And that was against strike drag! Just when it looked like jumping again and precious line could be gained, it had sounded into the abyss.

Once hooked up I had gunned *Sea Venture* in reverse, diesel fumes belching all over the angler and crew. Lee had collected some yardage but now it was straight up-and-down fishing with the giant marlin holding the upper hand, gaining line slowly but constantly. Snudger, my number one deckie, lit Lee yet another Camel. Snudger had rigged baits and wired Lee's fish for years and they were great mates.

"You okay, Boss?" he inquired.

"Just fine," Lee lied.

I could see that the years of hard drinking and hell raising were taking their toll. Lee's ten seasons had seen twelve granders weighed and at least another dozen or so tagged and released. But Glassell's 1953 all-tackle record of 1,560 pounds still eluded him.

"Could this be the one, Brazak?" he shouted over his shoulder to me. "Is this the one that'll stop me comin' back for more torture next year. Can't we just break that goddam record and get it over and done with so I can go home and never have to come back and look at your ugly face again?"

"Shut up and stop complaining," I yelled. "Anyone would think it's your first decent fish the way you're carryin' on."

"It's OK for you," Lee quipped. "I don't see too many of you guys in the chair."

Fair comment. Professional skippers rarely, if ever, take a

strike. But so I could relate to my angler's agony, I'd actually caught a couple of thousand pounders over the years and had some giant bluefin tuna - including an 830 pounder - almost rip my guts out in the Bahamas. I reckon sitting in that chair is like giving someone a $100 note and a baseball bat and telling them to bash you. Leave me outa that. I'd rather be in the tower any day.

Two hours now and still the stalemate. I could see that the constant pressure of the kidney harness was cutting into Lee's skin so it was time to change to a butt harness. I eased *Sea Venture* into reverse taking slight pressure off the fish. Changing the harnesses took a minute. Now he could fight the fish more comfortably. With my angler comfortable I nursed *Sea Venture* into forward gear and the pressure was back on.

"Hey, Brazakka - they always come up eventually don't they?"

"Come on Lee - you know the rules. Wind the line, pay the bills and shut up!"

"Gotcha." Another Camel. Lee danced his feet up and down on the footrest. They looked cold and wet. His circulation would have been nil. "Where's the blood?" he moaned.

After three hours it was time to try something different. "Ease the clutch back a touch. I'll circle east and see if we can get a better angle," I called.

With fish like this one, this is common practice and usually results in the marlin coming to the top. But it wasn't the case today. That big mother had her nose bogged down into the current a hundred fathoms down and she wasn't going to budge.

Two more hours and late into the afternoon I became concerned that we wouldn't get the fish before dark. I sure hoped we would, as navigating back to the safety of inside the reef wasn't my idea of fun at night. And staying out all night in the joggling seas wasn't what gamefishing was all about either.

I knew what was running through Lee's mind. He would contemplate breaking the fish off. It's late and we should be heading for home. Did he really need another grander? Of course he did. Marlin junkies always need another grander. Besides this could be Mrs. Big. He'd chicken out and make me make the decision. I did. With the sun about an hour away from disappearing into the sea, I made up my mind. I ran down from the tower and stood beside him. He wasn't looking real good.

"Listen, Lee. You've been on it for nearly five hours now mate and I suggest we 'sunset' it. Ease back on the drag, turn the clutch up about half a dozen turns and crank it back up to about ninety pounds of drag. Then there's one of four things that's going to happen. The line is going to break; the reel is going to explode; you're going to collapse in the chair, or the fish is going to come.

"When you sunset it, you're going to have a lot of drag there and the fish is not going to be able to pull at all so just hang on. When it gives you a bit - take it. She's probably hooked square in the jaw and is just going from side to side. I've tried every trick in the book and she's still wide awake."

Suggesting sunsetting a thousand pound plus fish to an exhausted angler is like asking a condemned man to sing 'New York, New York' in the electric chair as they throw the switch. Maximum clutch means the angler actually lifts the huge fish until either he, the line, the reel or the fish gives up. Whichever lasts the longest wins. In other words, no matter what - let's get home before sunset. Besides, Lee had reached the point of no return. There was no going back now. No thoughts of giving in. He had to know how big that fish was. After all, wasn't he the bloke who had told me that these huge fish can rob a man of his spirit and destine him to relive the fight in bars every now and then for the rest of his life?

It was time for the mumbles. Lee always had a chat with himself under his breath when it was getting close to the end and his back and legs were in diabolical pain. It was as if he was playing a part in a movie. But this was for real. And this fish was hurting worse than any of the others.

"Come on, Lee," he mumbled. "That fish is hurtin'. I'm hurtin'. But I gotta know."

Another hour and the sun was on the water and we were dangerously close to having to cut the fish off. But Lee hung in there and seemed to be winning although each crank of the handle was agony. I was glad it wasn't me lifting that slowly moving dead weight from the bottom of the ocean. But the reel hadn't blown up. The line was still intact. The fish hadn't come. And Lee was still alive … just.

Then Lee solved the problem for me. Suddenly he gathered line quickly. The fish was coming. He had turned it's head and now, way beyond the point of sheer exhaustion, he had to somehow gather line as quickly as the fish came to the surface.

Then she was there. I backed down on where she lay on the surface and Snudger took a couple of wraps on the wire. The boat was swamped as the huge tail reacted to the first gaff. Snudger secured the second gaff and it was over. Within moments the big fish was dead from sheer exhaustion.

"Now can I get out of this son-of-a-bitch?" Lee asked, unable to believe that he could finally leave the chair.

"Go for it," I said. "But do it slowly." Impatiently Lee struggled out of the chair and collapsed on the deck and had to be helped up.

Eleven hundred and forty-eight pounds. Not Lee's biggest but his last. He returned the following season with his family but didn't personally fish. Lee Marvin passed away in August 1987. He was buried in Washington with full military honors.

I am glad he was my friend.

BRAZAKKA

But now those days of killing big marlin just for the sake of it are long gone. Nowadays it is rare for any of my anglers to take a fish unless it is potentially the all-tackle world record. Besides, all of the really big fish are breeding females that are on the Reef that time of year to have their eggs fertilised as they lay them by the smaller males. Killing them for no special reason was senseless.

But there was the exception. One angler who had fished with me for years intended to take a big marlin and have a cast made of it in Cairns for his den back home in the States. But it had to be big ... at least a thousand pounds.

Which posed a problem. Seeing as I let all of my fish go, I only had the one deckie, and to kill a big fish, I needed two - one on the wire and one for the first gaff. I rang a fishing journalist mate of mine in Sydney and asked him if he'd like to come along for the ten days and act as gaff man if we got a big fish and get a story for his magazine into the bargain.

He jumped at it. And as it turned out, we had a day that none of us will ever forget. My journo mate from the big smoke got a terrific yarn so maybe it would be best if I let him tell you the story

A GRAND TALE
by
PAUL B. KIDD

It was a big fish. No, not big - huge ... well, by my standards anyway. And if it wasn't for the top half of it's man-sized sickle tail zigzagging the water about fifteen feet back from the bait, we probably wouldn't have known it was there at all as we were trolling 'blind' into the sun with the glare on the water. But it was there, and by the way it was crawling all over our scad bait, we were in for some hot action. I looked up at the skipper in the tower for a second opinion.

"It's a big bastard, Paul," Brazakka mumbled. "Hope it eats."

It did. And if we got it alongside the boat, it was my job to kill it. I was crewing on a special charter out of Cairns with my mate, Captain Dennis 'Brazakka' Wallace. I had met and fished with Brazakka twenty-five years earlier in a Cairns light-tackle tournament and we had become good friends. We retained our friendship over the years while pursuing our fishing careers but going in different directions. I chose to write and edit magazines about my passion, while Brazakka went on to become one of the world's great black marlin captains.

Brazakka and I kept in touch and whenever I was in Cairns or he was in Sydney, we'd get together for a beer. So it came as no great surprise when he rang and asked if I'd like to spend ten days with him out on the Great Barrier Reef during peak marlin time. Of course I would! But what's the catch?

Seeing as he hadn't killed a marlin in eight years and he required the services of only one deckhand to let them go, he was in a spot. His charter, a Texan, wanted to take a big fish. He had fished with Brazakka for five seasons and had released over a hundred fish, including a few that would have been more than a grand. This season he wanted to kill one and have it mounted on his wall. He figured that if the Japanese longliners could take 800,000 assorted billfish out of the ocean each year, then his one fish wasn't going to have a dramatic effect on their decline.

Seeing as Brazakka's deckie, Mark, would be busy on the leader wire getting the fish within range of a gaff, they would need a second man to perform the coup de grace. I would be that second man. This moment of mayhem is the most dangerous part of the catch. Bones are often broken, fish are lost, reputations smashed and wire and gaff men are often dragged over the side. I'd gaffed tiger and mako sharks up to 800 pounds off the NSW coast - and they are a handful, believe me - but the biggest marlin I'd ever gaffed would have been no bigger than about 300 pounds.

Brazakka explained that my home for the ten days would be the floating palace, the 120 foot *Achilles II,* the largest mothership in the fleet, with a replacement value of around $A12 million. Still, at upwards of $2,000 a day for up to three gamefishing boats and their charters at a time, you would expect the ultimate. Brazakka said that seeing as we were going to be the only boat living on it at the time, we had the *Achilles II* and its doting crew all to ourselves. I thought about it for a nanosecond and accepted. Running through the back of my mind of course, was the distinct possibility that they might not catch a whopper at all and my whorish services wouldn't be required. I could still get lots of pics and stories and live like a king at night on Battlestar Gallactica.

Yes, I'd love to go to the Great Barrier Reef.

After the three hour flight from Sydney to Cairns I took a float plane up the coast to where *Achilles II* sat like a satellite city inside the Number Five Ribbon Reef. It made Brazakka's fifty-four foot *Sea Venture*, which was tied alongside, look like a tender.

Brazakka was waiting on the back of *Achilles II* to meet me. "Say hello to Big Bill from Texas," he said, as he introduced us. Bill was a mountain of a man with shoulders like a padded-up gridiron player and a mitt like a leg of ham.

"How y'all doin?" he grinned, as he shook my hand until it hurt. "Brazakka tells me you're gonna gaff that big fish for me. It don't worry ya none, does it? Killin' one of 'em, ah mean?" He finally let go of my hand.

"No, not at all," I replied. "That's what I'm here for."

"Good," he exclaimed. "Me and my darlin' Connie have been comin' down here these past five years and I reckon it's time for me to get a mould of a big one I've caught and take it home for the den."

And so off we went. No time to unpack, just load my gear into my cabin and take off fishing. From where *Achilles II* was anchored we were about a mile to the gap in the reef and the open sea where the big marlin lived in the bottomless cobalt waters of the Coral Sea. Within half an hour of my arriving we had the baits out on the 130 pound outfits and ten minutes later we were hooked up on a small black around 300 pounds. Under normal circumstances I would be disappointed to go home after a day's fishing. But getting back to the *Achilles II* at night was a real treat - a chilled beer, fabulous food and a chat about the day's events. And there was plenty to talk about.

The first couple of days were good, with a few fish up to 400 pounds released. The fourth day was one of the best fishing days of my life. We had worked our way north and were fishing off the Number Ten Ribbon and the bite was hot. We got ten fish up, six of them bit, and we hooked up and released four. The biggest was around 800 pounds - a whopper by my standards but only a tiddler compared with what was to come.

It was on the fifth day that Mrs. Huge appeared behind the baits. She was lit up like a fire cracker; pectorals a stark white and her oil-barrel torso a myriad of fluorescent blue and white bars, something that they do when they are about to eat or mate. Brazakka turned the boat out of the sun so he could get a better look at the fish.

"Big bastard," he mumbled. That's about as excited as he got. For a bloke who loves a chat he's unusually quiet when the bite's on.

She took the bait and Brazakka gunned the boat ahead and hooked up. *Sea Venture* went nose first into the twelve foot swell with the huge marlin effortlessly peeling off line against the strike drag of sixty pounds. Big Bill had his work cut out just getting the rod from the gunwale to the chair unaided. At last he was settled and Mark buckled him up to the harness. Only now did I see why the big Southerner was held in such esteem for his angling skills. Bill's powerful legs and back combined to put pressure against the fish and gain line at every opportunity. But as much as Bill took, the big fish took it back. The acrobatics were spectacular. How anything that big could propel itself clear of the water was beyond me.

"How big?" I asked Brazakka.

"Eleven plus," he growled. And he'd know.

I stayed out of the way on the flying bridge. My gaffs were ready in the cockpit, secured to the stem of the fighting chair. Soon I would have to earn my keep. And so the fight continued, with the marlin staying fortunately on or near the surface, away from the sharks. Then she didn't jump anymore. She just bogged down flat out into the current about twenty metres below the surface with Brazakka full speed in reverse after her.

Two hours later and Big Bill was holding up pretty good. He could still manage a huge grin. "This is the hardest fish I ever fought," he cussed. "She just don't wanna die."

After two-and-a-half hours, it was time. The trace was up and Mark took a wrap in his double strength leather gloves and lifted the big fish toward the boat. I was beside him with my gaff ready.

"For Christ's sake, don't choke on me," Mark said. "No heroics. Just a neat shot in the shoulder."

By now all fifteen feet of the fish was coming and I got my first good look at it. I almost froze at the sheer size of it as its head with its beak like a baseball bat and eye the size of a bread and butter plate broke the surface in an attempt to leap out of the water at the back of the boat.

Until my dying breath I will never forget the look of defiance in her eye. My reflection seemed to disappear deep into it as I prepared to kill her. She was exhausted from the fight and as Brazakka inched the boat back Mark took bigger wraps on the trace. It was almost time for the kill. I readied my gaff. Another few inches and I would impale her and she would die. So close now. The water was pouring over the transom and into the cockpit as we reversed into the sea.

Now she was alongside, perfectly positioned for me to perform my duty. I steadied ...

"No," called the big Texan. "Cut her loose."

"What the fuck ...," I yelled.

"Don't argue," he bellowed. "Let her go."

Mark cut the wire and with one flick of her tail she disappeared into the abyss to have her babies. I turned to the big Texan, who was smiling from ear to ear. I looked up at Brazakka and he was smiling too.

Brazakka was a magnet for the rich and famous keen to fish with the gamefishing legend. But undoubtedly the most famous of the all was American Oscar-winning actor Lee Marvin who chartered Brazakka for twelve seasons. Together they weighed thirteen granders – the biggest 1320 pounds – and tagged at least a dozen more that would have made it.

"Build her and they will come" Brazakka's fifty-four foot *Sea Venture* was the first of her kind in Cairns, Australia with accommodation for four anglers, the captain, cook and two crew, and the range to fish as far north as Lizard Island. From day one the wild man in his yellow boat was fully booked every season.

Brazakka was the only Austrailian captain with security clearance
to take an American president big game fishing. Here he is with
Jimmy Carter after a day's fishing off Carins during which the
president tagged and released a sailfish.

Captain Bobby Brown

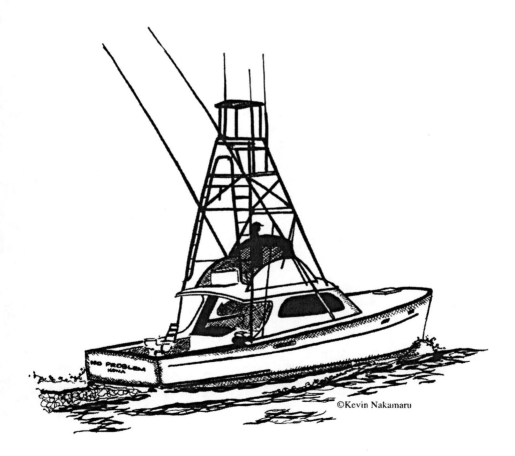

©Kevin Nakamaru

CAPTAIN BOBBY BROWN

Bobby Brown was born in Hilo on the Big Island of Hawaii. His fishing experience goes back so far that he can't remember a time before he fished. His family had a beach home in Kona where Bobby spent weekends and most of his summers and fished every chance he could. He landed his first blue marlin as an angler at the age of twelve on the *Miss Kona,* a boat owned by his neighbor. It was a 456 pound blue. When he was fourteen, Bobby and his brother, Monty, started taking a P-14 boat with a thirty-five H.P. Johnson offshore. They would take this fourteen foot runabout offshore and fish for blue marlin among the full-sized charter boats.

After graduating from high school Bobby studied mechanical engineering at California State Polytechnic College in San Luis Obispo. Bobby had spent the past couple of summers working for the Hawaiian Telephone Company as an equipment installer when Monty talked him into coming back to Kona where he said he could get him a summer job on one of the charter boats. It sounded pretty good to Bobby, so he headed back to Kona with the full intention of continuing his studies in California later that fall. He got a job onboard the single-screw, thirty-eight foot wooden hull *Mai Tai.* The owner of this boat was captain on a private boat as well and offered Bobby an opportunity to run *Mai Tai* as its captain. This had great appeal to Bobby, so he studied on his own and stood for the captain's license exam in Honolulu at the age of twenty-one. He passed on the first try and became the captain of the *Mai Tai* where he helped its owner build a charter business. Needless to say, returning to Cal Poly that fall didn't happen, it was put on hold indefinitely. At the time there were only twelve charter boats in

Kailua-Kona, and they were on moorings in Kailua Bay, an open roadstead, as the Honokohau Harbor was yet to be built.

During this time Bobby became friends with the actor Lee Marvin who fished with Bobby from time to time until Marvin bought his own boat. Even after this they remained close friends and spent much time together to talk about fishing over a few cocktails and dinners at the old Kona Steak House. In this same period Bobby's father acquired a fifty-five foot, single screw "haole sampan" that was called *Aukai*. The *Aukai* was a big improvement over the *Mai Tai* and so Bobby took the opportunity. They ran charters, entered fishing tournaments and even won the famous Henry Chee Award for the Hawaiian International Billfish Tournament in 1969. But Bobby also continued to fish commercially part time and used *Aukai*, which was set up with large fish boxes and live wells, to fish for yellowfin tuna, mahimahi, and wahoo, trolling with rod and reel on multi-day trips to the South Point area of the Big Island. To this day that area is virtually unfished by the local charter boats out of Kona even though it has some of the best fishing in the Hawaiian Islands.

In 1970 Bobby was offerd the job as captain of a forty-one foot Hatteras sport fisherman *Kona Seafari*. The family kept the *Aukai* and Bobby and Monty used it for commercial fishing when they each had time off from their full time jobs, Monty as a hotel manager at the Kona Inn and then Kona Surf hotels, and Bobby as captain of the *Kona Seafari*. The *Kona Seafari*, being a modern and fast, at the time, twin screw sportfisherman was a major improvement over the slow single screw boats Bobby had operated for the past four and a half years, and gave Bobby an opportunity to compete with the other more modern sportfisherman that were starting to show up in Kona. Bobby decided to put his efforts into chartering full time during this period and his father decided to sell the *Aukai*, but it is still being used as a charter boat in the islands. It was during this period that the charter business in Kona was growing and Bobby became one of the most sought after captains in the area. It was also on *Kona Seafari* that he caught his first grander, an 1,170 pound blue marlin on eighty pound test line, that, had the mate not hooked the fish for a novice angler from Canada, would still be the eighty pound test world record for Pacific blue marlin. It was at this time that Bobby began to fish for marlin and tuna on light tackle with a good friend and client from Los Angeles named Steve Zuckerman. Steve would charter the boat for several weeks during the peak of the marlin season and fish with twelve, sixteen, twenty, and thirty pound test line in search of a world record for either blue marlin or yellowfin tuna.

After about two years as captain of the Hatteras, a personal friend of Bobby's asked him to help put together a boat in San Diego. It was the thirty-one foot Bertram *High Flyer.* The friend made an offer that Bobby found impossible to refuse so he left the *Kona Seafari* and took the job which lasted from 1974 to 1975. When the boat was finished Bobby shipped it to Kona where it was the sharpest boat in the fleet at the time. Steve Zuckerman chartered *High Flyer* many times, and together he and Bobby set several world records, the first of which was the twelve pound test blue marlin world record, which was also the first blue marlin ever caught on twelve pound line.

It was also during this time that the world famous angler JoJo Del Guercio of Fort Lauderdale came through Hawaii and chartered the High Flyer on his way back to Florida from Australia. From that meeting a conversation ensued regarding Jo Jo's boat the thirty-seven foot Merritt *No Problem.* Bobby learned that the boat was available for sale as Del Guercio was building a new forty-three foot Merritt. Bobby called his friend and client, Haakon Nordass and told him of the opportunity with *No Problem.* Knowing what a great fisherman JoJo was, and knowing his worldwide reputation, Nordass offered to buy the boat, sight unseen. This was December 1975 and this world class Merritt sold on the spot for only $55,000. Bobby flew to Pompano Beach, Florida to refit the boat at Merritt's Boat and Engine Works and ship it back to Kona, and from 1974 until 1979 Bobby skippered it and built up its charter business. They fished a lot of light tackle, mostly fifty pound and less, and it was also during this time that they set the record for most marlin caught in a single year, 127, of which almost half were tagged and released, something unheard of in Kona where all of the marlin were put on the dock to be sold. In 1979 the owner of *No Problem* decided he wanted a bigger boat and sent Bobby to Florida and Merritt's Boat and Engine works to purchase a forty-three foot Merritt. That boat was also named *No Problem* and it spent its first year traveling around the Florida Keys, Cozumel, and the Bahamas. Steve Zuckerman chartered it and tied for second place with four other boats in the Cat Cay Tuna Tournament. No Problem split its time between Cat Cay and Bimini and caught six giant bluefin tuna that one month. Then Bobby took the new *No Problem* back to Merritts boat yard where they removed the tuna tower and prepared the boat for transshipment to Kona where he charter fished it until the end of 1983.

At this time Bobby was offered a job to find, and captain, a sportfisherman based in Rockport Texas that would fish the Gulf of Mexico, Mexico, Virgin Islands, and Venezuela as a regular circuit. The money was too good to turn down so he gave notice to the owner of the *No Problem* and went to Florida to look for a boat in January of 1984. They settled on a fifty-three foot Rybovich, *Pelstar,* and started fishing out of Rockport, Texas. Since he was no longer going to be available to captain the *No Problem*, the owner decided to sell it.

For two years *Pelstar* traveled along the Gulf Coast, fishing tournaments from Brownsville, Texas to South Pass, Louisiana, and then St. Thomas, Venezuela and Mexico. During the summer of 1985 the oil prices fell, and the owner of the *Pelstar*, being in the oil drilling business, had to put the boat up for sale. Bobby took *Pelstar* to Merritt boat yard to help the owner sell it. It was during this time, January 1986, that Bob Pernecky and Duane Zobrist, who had bought *No Problem* in Kona, contacted Bobby and asked him to return to Hawaii and get the charter business back on track after a couple of slow years. Bobby went back to Kona and ran the boat for him and built the charter business back up to where it had been. Then Penecky sent him to Florida to purchase a bigger boat that would be able to stay out for multi-day trips after the great fishing they had seen at South Point. He went off to Florida again, and working with the brokers at Merritt's Boat Yard, found a late model fifty-four Bertram which they purchased and named *No Problem*. Bobby remained in Florida for a few months outfitting the Bertram in preparation for getting it to Hawaii. But this time Bobby did not put the boat on a flatbed or ship for transport to Hawaii. He ran it on it's own bottom all the way. From Fort Lauderdale he took the boat to Pinas Bay and Tropic Star Lodge, Panama. There they caught several blue marlin and started a fishery that the local Panamanians didn't know they had during the winter months. Then they traveled up the west coast of Central America, for a few days of fishing before heading up to Newport Beach, California. Here the boat stayed while the winter storm season wound down in the northeast Pacific, and prior to the beginning of the tropical weather season in the eastern Pacific. With a crew of four and 2,200 gallons of fuel in containers on the deck plus the 1,400 gallons in the tanks, Bobby drove the new *No Problem* all the way to the Hawaiian Islands, an eleven day trip of 2240 nautical miles. In 1988 there was no GPS, just intermittent SAT NAV, so the crew used the old standby sextant, chronometer, and compass to back up the SAT NAV for their navigational work while crossing the Pacific. *No Problem*, with

Bobby Brown as its captain, found its way to its new home in Kona.

Then in 1990 Bob Pernecky decided to return the Bertram to Fort Lauderdale with the intention of buying a new and bigger boat. But when *No Problem* finally arrived in Florida, Pernecky decided to sell the boat and spend more time with his family. As soon as the word got out that *No Problem* was for sale, Larry Liebert, owner of the sixty foot Bertram *Miss Guided*, contacted Bobby to go to work for him. Bobby took the job and then permanently moved to Fort Lauderdale. *Miss Guided* fished the waters from St. Thomas, Venezuela, Panama, and Costa Rica in Bobby's first season as its captain. When Liebert decided he wanted to build a Merritt boat, he contracted for a sixty-five footer and Bobby flew back and forth from Panama and Costa Rica to Pompano Beach to oversee the building of the new *Miss Guided*. The new Merritt was designed for extended fishing trips to the coast of Panama and Costa Rica where dockage was not readily available and they would be "camping out" on the hook most of the time. In fact, when the boat left Florida, it was on it's own generator power until returning to Fort Lauderdale five to six months later as there was practically no dockage available with shore power in central America. The *MissGuided* spent several seasons fishing out of Panama and Costa Rica back when there were only a handful of American sportfisherman traveling to the area.

While still working for Larry Liebert, Bobby leased the forty foot Gamefisherman, the *French Look*, for him to fish Madeira in July and August of 1995. They caught several large blue marlin, the largest of which was better than 1,100 pounds and was released. Bobby stayed onboard *Miss Guided* until it was sold in February of 1996. 1996 found Bobby leasing the forty-six foot Merritt *Nitso* for Earl Burke, the Texas oil man who previously owned the *Pelstar*, to go to Isla Mujeres, Mexico, in February, and March for the sailfish season, even though it was a couple of months earlier than when most boats traveled there for the sailfish. It was in February that they found the large numbers sailfish schooling and balling bait. The first day they found the bait and large schools of sails (Bobby almost turned away thinking they were just bonito before realizing that the splashing was from sailfish feeding on the huge schools of sardines under flocks of frigate birds) his anlgers caught forty-four sails in a two and a half hour period and could have caught a lot more. They quit fishing at 4:30 with anglers too tired to wind any more. At the time this was the record for the Cancun area. There were only a handful of boats there then, but within a couple of days of the word getting out, another dozen boats from Florida showed up. The early January and February fishery has continued on since then.

In the first half of 1966 *French Look* fished throughout the Canary Islands and Madeira until July. Then in October Bobby was hired by Wayne Huizenga, Jr. to be captain of his fifty-three foot Viking, *Fonda Fishing,* delivering it from Atlantic City to Ft. Lauderdale. They fished throughout the Bahamas in most of the BBC tournaments, winning a couple of them, then on to St. Thomas, Panama, and Costa Rica, with a few trips to Isla Mujeres and Cancun, Mexico. In 2000 the Huizengas sold the Viking and purchased a custom built fifty-seven foot Island Boat Works sportfisherman, with plans to go to St. Thomas, Venezuela, Panama and Costa Rica. However, while in St Thomas on Sept. 11, 2001, the decision was made to return to Fort Lauderdale and await the outcome of the terrorist attacks on the World Trade Center. The painful decision was made by the Huizengas to take a break from world travels for sportfishing and stay close to home and family for a few years. The boat was sold later in 2001. Fonda Huizenga established several women's world records while fishing with Bobby Brown including a 350 pound Atlantic blue marlin on twelve pound test in the Cape Verde Islands, and the eight pound Pacific blue marlin record (180 pounds) while fishing in Costa Rica.

In 2001 Bobby became a licensed yacht broker at Merritt's Boat and Engine Works Brokerage on a part time basis. In that same year he started as captain on *Cutnail*, a fifty-five foot Viking owned by Ft. Lauderdale real estate developer Terry Stiles. In 2003 Stiles purchased the new *Cutnail*, a fifty-eight foot Merritt. In it they fish Isla Mujeres, Mexico, the Bahamas, Turks and Caicos Islands and St. Thomas. Bobby remains a consultant and frequent captain to the Huizenga family.

Bobby Brown has established many world records for himself and for many others. Some have been broken and some still stand. Perhaps the most important one, which has stood since 1982, is the all-tackle and 130 pound test world record Pacific blue marlin which was caught in Kona onboard *No Problem* and weighed in at 1376 pounds.

THE UNDERWATER WIREMAN'S CLUB
by
BOBBY BROWN

As if the thrill of fighting an eight hundred pound marlin, blue or black, doesn't give a captain, mate or angler enough excitement to fill a lifetime, hardly anything beats the added adrenaline rush of having one of the crew go overboard during the battle. This does not happen frequently, but it does happen from time-to-time, and when it does, nothing compares to the danger and all out stupefying sensory overload of trying to retrieve that individual before something tragic occurs. I've had three such events in my life, all of which were life altering experiences that I will never forget and that I hope never happen again. All of these episodes happened in Kona, Hawaii, one of the world's leading destinations for big game marlin fishing.

In the summer of 1975, I was the captain of the thirty-seven Merritt named *No Problem*. The boat's owner was Haakon Nordaas, a very successful homebuilder from Minnesota who had purchased it from the world famous angler, JoJo Del Guercio, and had it shipped from Florida to the Big Island. My angler this day was a gentleman from California named Steve Zuckerman who had chartered me for a month each year for the past several years. Steve was possibly the most avid seeker of light-tackle, line-class world record marlin at the time, and in fact held a number of world records which he earned during those summers aboard *No Problem*. My first mate and wire man was Mike Benham, the gaff man and second mate was John Shamel.

This was a day like many others, fishing the hundred fathom ledge off Kaheole Point in Kona which was known as "The

Grounds". The current was from the south to the north which created an upwelling on the southwest side of the ledge. This caused small fish and plankton to appear in the upwelling which in turn attracted the live bait, the kawakawa, skipjack tuna, and frigate mackerel. These in turn attracted many species of game fish. The bait was active, the birds were working all over the place and conditions looked perfect. We were fishing with live bait on twenty pound tackle with a 035 music wire leader and looking for a world record in this line class. The seas were calm with a light swell, actually perfect conditions for what we were trying to do.

Soon enough we hooked the fish we had been looking for. It appeared to be well in excess of 300 pounds and certain to be a twenty pound test world record blue marlin at the time. We had no doubt. Steve was on his game as a highly experienced and skilled angler. He and the crew of the Merritt worked like a well-oiled machine. Mike had many years of experience as a wireman in the cockpit, and what he may have lacked in physical size he made up for in skill and quickness. John had the versatility to be either wireman or gaffer, and I had skippered many a sportfish boat in similar circumstances and come up with several world records. On this day we were the dream team of the fleet, totally prepared for the task at hand.

My preference is always to move the boat and the fish in a way so as to bring the fish along side the boat. I never want it directly behind the transom. But this is big game fishing and what we want sometimes is not what we are going to get. This was one of those times, and the fish was directly behind the center of the transom with me backing down at full speed. The boat would back up the swells, come off the top and pick up speed as it surfed down the other side. Then when it hit the trough it would slow considerably before continuing its way over the next swell. This continued for about twenty minutes as Steve brought the marlin closer and closer. I stood on the bridge facing the transom with my back to the console. With transmissions in reverse and throttles to the wall, I watched everything my angler and mates did. It seemed that whenever I tried to get the boat alongside the fish, it would make a slight turn and end up directly behind the transom, again swimming away from us. I saw the swivel break the surface and watched as Mike took a wrap on the leader. The boat skidded down the back of the swell enabling Mike to get a good second wrap on the leader. Then the universe came together in a most unfortunate way. As Mike got the second wrap, the boat slowed considerably at the bottom of the trough, the marlin, feeling the increasing pull on the leader, became airborne going away from the boat. He could not have been much more than ten feet from the transom as he jumped high into the air and Mike Benham, who was about five and a half feet tall and might have weighed one-forty soaking wet, came right out of the cockpit with his hand still firmly wrapped in the wire leader. All I saw after this was Mike's feet sticking up from above the covering board and headed into the drink. My heart raced and blood pounded in my ears as I watched his feet disappear and realized that I was about to back over him with no hope of stopping in time.

My angler and first mate stood frozen with their mouths agape watching as Mike disappeared. I stopped thinking and acted instinctively. I can't even say today that any clear thoughts or images came into my head. There was just Mike heading under the boat, and me jamming the gear shift levers into forward with the throttles still pegged to the wall. Then I instinctively pulled back to neutral as the boat continued on its backward course. It's a miracle that the gear box didn't blow all to hell, but thankfully those twin disk transmissions were built to be shifted in and out of gear at 80% power. I felt the props go from reverse to forward to neutral, but I did not feel them bump up against anything. No one spoke or screamed. We were all just too stunned to do anything. Steve still had the marlin on the line as it took off again dumping line and heading west. We all looked around the boat for signs of Mike's body or at least pieces of it. We looked for blood in the water, but we could see nothing. Now another realization hit us. Had Mike been knocked unconscious and sunk to the bottom? That sounded like an idea that had some possibilities. We looked behind the boat and from side to side but saw no signs of our wireman.

A feeling came over me that I was about to realize the worst experience of my fishing life. I was beginning to believe that there was no hope. I was thinking about the abject misery that Mike's family and friends would have to endure at the news of his unfortunate fate. All these negative thoughts had entered my mind and were just about to take over my entire consciousness when I looked out forward of the boat and saw my first mate's head pop through the surface. His eyes were as big as saucers as he began treading water about sixty feet away. I did a double take. Oh my God! Had Mike actually survived being run over by the twin props? Was he actually going to live to wire another day? This was too much good news to bear, but there was no time to waste. I placed the gear shift levers into forward and idled alongside where Mike was treading. I called down to him and he said he was OK, not injured in the least. Relief washed over me at this good news

We hauled Mike into the boat and checked him out. It looked like he was fine. He told me that he remembered being pulled overboard and having the boat back over him. His thoughts paralleled our own, and he too was certain that he was a goner. But as he went under the water and the boat backed over him, he said that all he could remember was a huge swirl of bubbles pushing him straight down, under and past the spinning props. The best we could figure was that when I jammed the gear shift levers into forward and then to neutral, it set up a reaction that created a downward push with all those bubbles. We examined Mike and found no bruises, but the evidence that he had been run over was still there as the blue paint from the Merritt's bottom was all over his clothing.

About a half hour later the marlin broke off, but we were happy just to be returning to port all in one piece.

MIKE'S SECOND TRIP OVERBOARD
by
BOBBY BROWN

On another occasion we were fishing off Keahole Point with Mike and John as the mates and Dick and Kay Mulholland, orange growers from California, were our anglers. We were going for a line class world record for blue marlin using twenty pound test line with live bait when the bite came. It was a black marlin, I believe every bit of 300 pounds. Black marlin usually behave quite differently from blues in the way they run and jump when they're hooked. You might see a blue marlin running and jumping, greyhounding in and out of the water and usually moving in one direction trying to escape the predator that has him hooked. A black marlin sometimes behaves this way too, but more often will make more vertical jumps and not the long greyhounding jumps that the blue marlin makes. Dick had a good hook in this marlin and had fought it well. He had it up to the boat in about twenty minutes. The fish was still green and jumping and thrashing right next to the boat, but since it was already at the side of the boat, Mike did what he was supposed to do and went for the leader. He took a double wrap on the leader trying to get it under control. The fish began another jump and was just coming out of the water when John reached over to tag it with one of the old fashioned Marine Fisheries four foot wooden tag sticks. I believe the shock of the tag in its side caused the marlin to convulse or give an extra kick which sent it high into the air while falling back towards the boat and John. John could not get the tag stick out of the fish and was still holding onto it as it thrashed violently in midair. At this point I believe the stick was pushing into the side of the fish pretty hard and was a great source of either fear or anger for the marlin. The extra kick carried the marlin up and over the transom. John ducked down to get out of the way, still holding onto the tag stick, and the next thing I saw was this very healthy sized black marlin soaring over top of John, and into the boat. John was knocked down as the fish sailed by, landing on top of him and the drink box.

I stood on the bridge stunned by what I was seeing, and hoping that no one would be injured or killed by this raging animal. From my position on the bridge all I could see was the tail of the fish sticking out from under the cabin overhang. The rest of its body was completely engulfed in the cabin. I think a lesser wireman might have cleared out and let the marlin do its damage. The dangers of a green marlin inside a boat are well known. They can not only injure or kill someone, but they can also make a huge mess out of the boat.

Mike still had the wraps around his hand and had the presence of mind to try to yank it out of the cabin while John, who was partially under the fish, tried to push it away. Somehow, and I'll never know how, that fish flopped back onto the deck and a moment later, with a mighty kick and Mike's guidance, it vaulted off the boat and back into the water.

With all the excitement and fast paced action, Mike may have forgotten about the leader wire wrapped around his hand. He turned around to say something to John but, as the marlin cleared the side of the boat, Mike was hauled overboard with it. As was the case with his prior launch, Mike disappeared for a few seconds and all I could see was Mike headed overboard and into the water. He disappeared for a few seconds and again I didn't know if he had been drowned, or what had happened. The line had parted and he was no longer attached to the boat. It would not have been out of the question for him to have been wrapped in the leader wire and dragged down with the marlin. The visions of what those possibilities might have been were haunting.

But only a few seconds later Mike bobbed to the surface. We hurriedly picked him up and he was unharmed. Added to that good luck was the fact that the boat had sustained very little damage. The high gloss varnish on the drink box had been scraped up and now was a bit duller than before, but all-in-all everyone was safe and no worse off for the adventure. Also in the plus column for this episode was the fact that, unlike the blue earlier in the summer that got away clean, we could record this event as a tag and release. Some T&Rs come at a higher price than others!

THE DAY I JOINED THE CLUB
by
BOBBY BROWN

During 1971 and 1972, I was the captain of the forty-one foot Hatteras named *Kona Seafari*, fishing off of the Kona coast of the Big Island of Hawaii. At the time I usually had a single mate in the cockpit, except for when we were light tackle fishing, and then we would bring a second mate along. When we were fishing with heavy tackle (in those days that meant one hundred thirty and eighty pound gear) I would run the boat from the bridge and, when the mate had control of a fish on the wire, I would come down off the bridge and either gaff or tag and release the fish.

This one day in the summer of 1971 we got a good hook in a blue marlin of around 300 pounds. Very soon we saw that this was a squirrely fish, one that was very active in the water, running and jumping, doing whatever it could to try and throw the hook and gain its freedom. It had been a relatively short fight and the fish was still green when we brought it to the boat.

In those days our gaffs would be cleated off on each side of the cockpit. Our technique had not evolved the way it has today and we did not know any better. Since that time we have learned that ideally the gaff rope should be attached somewhere at the center of the transom. The best setup we have been able to come up with is to fix our flying gaffs to the fighting chair stanchion in the center of the cockpit. The post is keel-mounted and strong enough to withstand any amount of force, and its location gives us the flexibility to move freely in either direction toward the fish. But back in those days we had not figured this out.

So here we were with our two gaffs cleated off on either side and, as the angler brought the fish up, it made a couple of jumps at the side of the boat. This fish was still feisty and green and fighting like crazy. When I saw my mate take a wrap on the leader, I assumed he had the fish under control. I placed one engine in neutral and kept the other in gear and quickly came off the bridge to help. As my mate held on to the fish and tried to get it under control, it continued to jump near the transom. I grabbed the nearest gaff and, when the marlin came around the corner and right under me, I stuck it. With this action the fish went ballistic and bucked and jumped wildly. The gaff pole pulled off the head as it was designed to do, and the fish was at the end of the gaff line before I could get a wrap on the cleat. As this was happening, I saw my mate's glove still wrapped in the leader go past my head. Fortunately his hand was not still in the glove. When the marlin got to the end of the gaff line, about thirty feet back then, it turned and came back around the transom and up to the other side of the boat. As the line was still on the cleat in the corner of the cockpit, and I still had not been able to get a wrap on the cleat to shorten the length of the line, the line was now beginning to pin my angler to the fighting chair. I sprang into action trying to relieve the tension of the gaff rope against my angler's chest, but in doing so I got between the rope and the transom. I was trying to yank the rope away from the angler and force the fish to come back around.

Everything between the line and the transom was at risk of being caught in the line as the marlin pulled tight on the gaff rope and moved back away from the transom. As the marlin headed away from the boat the line pulled tight against the back of my knees. I created little resistance as the marlin continued on its course and launched me out of the boat.

When I landed in the water the first thing I thought about was that I was swimming with a marlin that was bigger than me, he was stuck and bleeding, and fighting for his life. I did not kid myself,

I knew I was in extreme danger. The marlin was tethered to the boat, so any hopes of it swimming off could be forgotten. I looked over at him only a few feet away thrashing back and forth and coming straight at me. My heart was racing and my thoughts came in quick bursts, but I did not panic. I swam as fast as I knew how to get away from the boat. I only prayed that the gaff would remain stuck in the marlin as the boat moved slowly in forward. The marlin came at me like a shot. Its primordial instincts told it that I was a danger to it that must be dealt with. He was just about to deal with it in his way when the gaff line came taught again and slowly dragged him out of reach of me. In those few seconds when I realized that it could do me no harm, a wave of relief washed over me. I had come face to face with this awesome predator, but had escaped any injury by only the slightest few inches of the gaff line I had attached to him.

It was good to be free of the marlin but the excitement was not completely over. There was blood in the water which can create all kinds of other problems. Fortunately there were other boats in the area and my friend, Freddie Rice, who was watching this whole thing take place from his boat *Malia,* came over at full speed to rescue me. As he was on his way over I collected my wireman's glove and the gaff pole that had slipped loose. Freddy dragged me out of the water to safety while on board the Hatteras my mate had the boat stopped and the fish completely subdued. I joined the Underwater Wireman's Club that day and as long as I live I will never forget the experience.

As a result of having gone through this, my gaff lines are just long enough to allow the gaff man to reach as far as he can around the entire cockpit while the line is attached to the fighting chair stanchion, and not the thirty feet allowed by the IGFA. Ideally, a cleat centered on the transom below the covering board would be best, but on most of today's luxury sportfishing yachts it isn't quite possible and the stanchion is the best alternative.

DOUBLE DOUBLES AT KALEA
by
BOBBY BROWN

In 1987 the waters around Kona were teaming with marlin, tuna, wahoo and predators of another type: sportsmen seeking the thrill and challenge of big game fishing. They wanted to compete to see who was the best. They entered all the tournaments and they spent big bucks to make their mark in big game fishing circles. At that time one of the most avid seekers of world records was my friend Steve Zuckerman, an angler who chartered me for two weeks to a month each year to go after the big boys. Steve was a light tackle fisherman, and together we captured no fewer than twenty line class world records for marlin, tuna and spearfish.

An area that was fished less frequently at the time, compared to the amount of lines dragged through the waters just off Kona, was called Kalea, or South Point, about fifty miles to the south. We had a feeling that the bite might be on in the area so Steve said let's give it a try. We anticipated rougher waters than we were used to near Kona so we decided to abandon the light tackle and see what might happen with our 130 gear. In our forty-three foot Merritt, *No Problem*, we headed south early in the morning. I had my son Robbie, who was seven years old at the time, onboard along with Steve's son, Will, who was about the same age. They were close buddies who always enjoyed fishing with the grown-ups. My mates onboard were Doug Haigh and Fran O'Brien. Because South Point was such a long haul, we planned this trip as an overnighter. While it was our intention to release whatever marlin we caught, a friend of mine who was commercial fishing in the area was standing by just in case we caught a marlin that would not survive, and then we would transfer it over to his boat as he was planning on returning to Kona that night. We certainly did not want to kill a marlin and then waste it by staying out all night and having it rot on the deck.

Our lines went in about ten o'clock. We had passed the southernmost point of the island and were no longer in the lee. The wind was stiff and it was not long before we decided that it might be a little too rough out here for the boys. We decided to return to the lee, when we suddenly raised our first marlin. We didn't like that we were in such sloppy water but Steve fought the fish well and in just a few minutes we tagged it, called it at 375 pounds, and released it healthy. We then headed north to get back into the lee of the island.

Almost immediately upon returning to the calm water we hooked up again, only about a half mile from shore. This time it was a double header. Steve and I and our mates were a great team. One marlin was held off while Steve fought the first one in. We tagged it, called it 250, and released it healthy. Then Steve fought the second marlin to the boat, we tagged it and figured it to be around 400 pounds. Sadly the fish rolled over, and we were not able to resuscitate it, so we gaffed it and brought it into the boat. I called that friend of mine who was commercial fishing nearby and he said that he was heading back to Kona later in the day and he agree to take the dead marlin back with him. That way we could continue with our plan to stay out overnight.

We trolled north for a short while, trying to make up some of the distance between ourselves and our friend in the commercial boat, and get closer to the spot we were going to anchor in for the night. But very soon we had another bite. This fish looked very big and excitement was high onboard *No Problem*. As we were clearing the lines we got bit again, our second double header of the day! The first fish was a real good sized marlin, bigger than anything we had seen all day. The second fish looked quite a bit smaller. However, the first marlin pulled off after a few minutes, so Steve took the rod with the second fish on it. The fight lasted about thirty-five minutes, but we were not able to revive the marlin when we tried to release it, so had to put it in the boat along with the other marlin from earlier in the day. We were slightly bummed because we knew that the one that got off was even bigger than this one and we were guessing this one could be well over 600 pounds.

We had fished for most of the day and our friend in the commercial boat had long since headed back to Kona. We did not want to waste our nice catches so we scrapped our plans to stay overnight and headed back to Kona too. After all, we had hooked five marlin, tagged two, and missed several others. By any measure it had been a good day.

We returned to the Kailua-Kona town pier just after sunset and tied up to the weigh station. Much to our surprise the marlin that we guessed to be 400 pounds when we tried to release it turned out to be 680 pounds and the bigger one was 818 pounds. And they weren't even the biggest fish we had encountered that day.

Soon the word got out and everyone came down to the dock. They heard that Kalea was hot and the following day we returned to South Point, but we were not alone. Hearing of our success the day before, several other boats decided to give it a try. We caught two marlin ourselves that day and most of the other boats were successful too.

* *

South Point had always been a popular spot for me. During my part time commercial fishing days on our family boat, *Aukai*, I frequently fished in that area mostly for tuna and wahoo. It was on one of my trips back from that area that I made a discovery that changed the way I fished for yellowfin tuna (ahi) for a long time to come. In truth you could say that it was out of either laziness or exhaustion that I made this amazing discovery.

Heading north after several days of fishing, we were looking forward to getting back onto solid ground in Kona. Our thoughts were more on heading toward port than anything else but we left the lines in just in case something might happen. On the way up I found a school of spotted dolphins, a common sight in those waters. I didn't do much more than notice them as I continued north. My boat moved ahead of and at an angle to the school, and I didn't give it another thought until we got a solid hit from a yellowfin tuna. We brought in our prize and continued on our trek north. Again we trolled out in front of the school and again we hooked up. We became very suspicious that something was happening that we should pay close attention to.

On subsequent trips out, whenever we saw a school of these spotted dolphins we would drag our lines out in front of them and invariably we would catch yellowfin tuna. Very soon we determined that this was a phenomenon we could rely upon. We studied it, and found out that this was something the commercial tuna seine fleet based out of San Diego had known about and had been capitalizing on for a very long time. What we found out was happening was that the porpoises drove bait out and to the surface. Obviously wherever there is bait there is bound to be some kind of fishing to be had. The tuna were following the schools of porpoises because they too knew that the bait would be chased to the surface. All we had to do was to be ready with our lines, which we modified with small leaders and small jet lures that we trolled at a long distance behind the boat, to hook them up.

We used this technique many times, and, of all the commercial fishermen on the Big Island, we were catching more tuna than anybody. It had been our intention to keep this a big secret and we even went so far as to drive a long distance, a two hour drive to the auction house in Hilo, which opened at 5:00 AM, to sell our fish just so the competing commercial fishermen would not get wise to our system.

But good secrets like this do not stay secret for long and within a short time after our initial discovery, the word got out and the majority of the commercial fisherman in their small boats had learned about it too. Our advantage did not last for long, but we continued to use the technique for as long as we continued to fish for tuna, and the Kona fleet still fishes the porpoise schools in the same way today, along with the commercial fisherman using green sticks and hand lines.

Jay Debaubian poses with his all tackle world record 1376 pound blue
marlin caught on board *No Problem* in Kona, Hawaii. This record
has endured since Memorial Day 1982. Standing opposite is
Captain Bobby Brown with mate Doug Haigh.

Captain Bobby Brown stands in the cockpit of *No Problem* checking out the 1376 pound world record blue marlin. This photo shows a perspective of just how big this fish was.

Captain Bobby Brown pilots the thirty-seven foot Merritt *No Problem* through the waters off Kona, Hawaii. This boat and its crew set many world records including the largest ever IFGA-legal blue marlin.

Captain
Kevin Nakamaru

©Kevin Nakamaru

CAPTAIN KEVIN NAKAMARU

Kevin Nakamaru was born and raised in Kona, Hawaii where his passion all of his life was fishing. He was hooked at an early age when his mom caught her first marlin when he was three years old. With his parents and three sisters he fished for tuna and marlin in their family boat in the calm waters off Kona. He caught his first marlin when he was nine and his first big tuna when he was ten.

His mom and dad were active members of trolling clubs including the Hawaii Big Game Fishing Club and the IGFA. All the fishing they did was by the rules. Even following the tournament rules, Kevin's parents' fishing resulted in a number of records for Kevin's mom. In 1975 she caught a 565 pound Blue Marlin on fifty pound test and a 231 pound yellowfin tuna on eighty. In 1976 she broke her own tuna record with a 250 pounder. It was during those years that Kevin's foundation for fishing was being set for the fishing to come.

After graduating from high school, Kevin attended college in Colorado where he tied flies and guided trout fishing on the famed San Juan River for trophy trout in New Mexico. During his summers he fished Kona, either working on charter boats or often fishing alone on his dad's boat.

One of his most notable catches as an angler came during a summer while night fishing for swordfish and tuna with Capt. Freddy Rice on the *Ihu Nui*. This time he caught a 829 pound thresher shark on 130 pound test. It would have been the all tackle record had they had a crew that night. What happened was that Freddie and Kevin were alone fishing. When the thresher struck, Freddie had to drive the boat while Kevin pulled in the sea anchor and cleared the other lines. In the time it took to do all that, the rod had been left in the rod holder for too long to make the catch IGFA legal. This thresher was the largest ever caught on rod and reel anywhere in the world and still stands as the Hawaiian and Pacific record.

After graduating from Fort Lewis College with a degree in Fine Art, Kevin took a year to travel and fish, and to see some of the famed spots he had read about and dreamed of all of his life. One of these spots was the Great Barrier Reef off of Australia's Queensland coast. His luck was good when he got a job with Capt. Peter Wright on the *Duyfken* the following year. This was the opportunity of a lifetime for Kevin. It was a time when all of the base skills that he had learned could be polished by learning Peter's world class techniques. Their most notable catches during the three seasons they fished together were black marlins weighing 1,210, 1,188, and 1,020 pounds. They won the Dunk Island Classic three years in a row, and in 1994 won or placed in every major tournament held in Queensland including winning the Lexus and Lizard Island tournaments.

Kevin often traveled with Peter during these years. One of the best trips he made was to Bimini, Bahamas, to fish for bluefin tuna off Cat Key. Their last day there they caught a 971 tuna off Sandy Cay that was the Bahamas record at that time. He also spent a few days in North Carolina where he tagged forty-six bluefin tuna in three days.

The dream to travel and see the world took Kevin to Madeira, Portugal where he ran the thirty foot express *Pesca Grossa* for five years during Madeira's peak seasons. He weighed a 1,075, and an 1,188 Atlantic blue at a time when catching granders was common in that area. He released a number of fish that taped out well into the mark. They caught a number of big eye tuna including several in the 300 pound class and one that weighted in at 330 pounds. They caught many fish over 700 pounds in the same day.

On June 26, 1996 angler Ken Corday caught an 1,100 pound fish and another of 750 pounds and another one of 550 pounds. On the same day a year later, and nearly to the hour, he caught one that weighed 1,170 pounds. Kevin says, "What made the experience even better was catching those quality fish for all the great anglers we got to fish with. We learned a lot and got to spend time with fishermen with the same spirit for fishing the next best spot. The culture and the beauty of the island was so memorable."

Once the fishing slowed in Madeira, Kevin returned home to Kona to pursue a childhood dream of skippering a Merritt. When the *Northern Lights* came up for sale, Kevin and Terry Fohey bought it. They share a unique friendship centered on the same goal . . . enjoying the fishing on the way to the next 1,000 pound fish.

It was on the *Northern Lights* that Kevin's most significant catch was made. He was the first angler, captain or crew to catch three thousand-pound billfish of different species by landing an 1,115 Pacific Blue on April 6, 2000. This was the Triple Crown of Granders when added to the grander black marlins he caught in Australia and Atlantic blue marlins caught in Madeira.

In the summer of 2005 an important record was made onboard *Northern Lights*. With Kevin as Captain, and Terry Fohey in the chair, they caught and released eight blue marlin on one day beating the previous Kona record of six in one day. Two days later they tied their eight-catch record again but lost the ninth at the boat.

The foundation for fishing that Kevin was given by his parents from such a young age has led him to numerous notable catches, including over twenty billfish and tuna world records and numerous tournament wins. His love of fishing and continued learning has kept him on the cutting edge of fishing. Kevin says, "I really enjoy the charter fishing here in Kona because there are so many talented captains and crews that it provides us with a great opportunity to develop and learn from each other. I feel fortunate to have seen a lot of great fishing early in my life and am ready to face the biggest challenge ahead, raising my children."

Today Kevin spends most of his time in Kona charter fishing on the *Northern Lights*, traveling for two weeks at a time and raising his family with his Madeiran wife, Elizabete, and their two daughters Gabriella and Juliana.

MY FIRST SEASON IN MADEIRA
by
KEVIN NAKAMARU

There is a chapter of my fishing career that taught me a great deal about something I have grown up loving to do. Fishing has been such a big part of my life, and I have grown up by learning those lessons while fishing all over the world. The first season that I fished the small Portuguese island of Madeira, I went there to experience the great fishing and left there with a lot more than I ever imagined.

News of the incredible big fish traveled the professional fishing world like wildfire. The fishery that was discovered by Roddy Hays was proving itself to be more than a fluke. The incredible numbers of big fish were staggering. That season of 1994 finished with stats that have never really been seen since. Those fortunate enough to be in Madeira at that time had angling experiences that will stand out for years to come.

I was fishing in my home waters of Kona, Hawaii with Scott Levin on the *Sea Baby III* for the summer. Scott and I had fished the Great Barrier Reef with Peter Wright the three seasons before. All we heard during that time were stories from anglers and journalists that were calling the fishing in Madeira the Jurassic Park of marlin fishing. One of our anglers that summer was Tracy Melton, and he shared the same desire to experience what everyone was talking about.

After a satisfying summer in Kona, Scott and I headed for the Barrier Reef. We were not surprised to have heard the same Madeira "buzz" there. Our wheels began to spin faster when we heard the news that our friend Tracy had gotten to Madeira and had caught the first grander on standup tackle with Roddy Hays. Tracy was hooked on the action, but when he tried to book for the following year, he found that there were no openings. The Madeira boats were booked for two years out. In order to see the great fishing of Madeira we were going to have to get our own boat and get it there.

We focused on finding a boat and began to dream. That was the easy part! I soon learned that coordinating all of this in a foreign country with all of the planning and politics would push me to limits I never imagined.

Tracy had found a thirty foot boat in the city of Villamora on the Portuguese mainland. The boat was built in Australia and fished most of her life in the Azores where it had done very well. It was advertised as a fish-catching boat and was a fully reconditioned vessel with rebuilt engines. Once I got there I realized that it would take more than some paint and simple maintenance to get me to the fishing grounds. Within five minutes I realized that I may have made a big mistake and that it was going to take every bit of the three months I had reserved to get the boat to a satisfactory standard.

I stood there taking it all in and not really knowing where to start. The boat needed a full paint job. The lawn chair tower that was on it had to be taken off, and when I looked at the engines I saw that the extent of the rebuilt engines was probably a impeller change and some hose repair with a foot of duct tape. She had fished the challenging waters of the Azores for years and it showed inside and out. We named her the *Pesca Grossa* meaning 'big fish'. She needed a lot of work, but she had the proper papers to charter, and she was going to have to do for us if we were going to legally charter her.

This daunting task was made more difficult by the fact that I didn't speak Portuguese. After two months of just plain hard work, putting in fourteen hour days and working alone in the south Portugal sun, I began to make some progress. With a very limited budget we ordered a new tower, chair and electronics. We had them shipped to Madeira where we would finish the job by putting the new gear on a fresh boat, with plenty of time until the bite came on in a month or so.

What made the days shorter were the lunches of fresh fish at my friend Manuel's restaurant where I didn't need to order. He would bring me Portuguese dishes of fish that he had bought off of the boats that morning. It took time to get used to the fact that the boatyard shut down for a minimum hour lunch, and that wine or a few beers had to accompany the long lunch hour.

The adventure of getting the boat to Lisbon from Villamora is a story in itself. The delivery on the truck was barely successful and the boat made it to Madeira with some incredibly lucky events. Tracy met me in Lisbon where we put the boat on the ship. We would meet Scotty in Madeira and I would get a couple days rest while we waited for the boat to show up in Funchal.

The long days working on the boat wore me out. The difficult days seemed to continue getting worse, and then the worst thing of all happened: the fish started biting early. We sat waiting for a boat that needed to be fully outfitted while the fish started to really come on strong. The granders we were dreaming of were out there a month early and we could feel the pressure to get moving. Until this point I had ridden my hopes and dreams. I was so worn out that I began to feel no inspiration or confidence that we would ever start fishing. At this point the reality of all the work and preparation that we took for granted as mates for years started to sink in, and the title Captain held new meaning to us.

We worked on our charter paper work and worked hard on the boat. In seven long days we were ready to tie double lines on our rods. The bite had been on for three weeks and we looked forward to getting out there. We had one day to shake things down and we started our first charter the following day. I remember sitting with Scotty on the boat with the rods finally out and the lures ready to go, and wondering where we were going to get the energy to actually fish, much less with clients on a boat and with no proper shake down.

When we finally set sail for our maiden voyage, we realized that the fuel tanks were dirty and they ran so rough that on the night before our first charter we were going to have to empty the tank of all the fuel and start fresh. We got it cleaned out at 1:00 AM and were ready to go get fuel and start fishing our first client in the morning.

We ran our first charter and made it through the day. We saw one nice fish that tried the lure and left. We needed alignment and a number of other tune-ups, so I wasn't surprised the fish didn't stick with it. Our first ten day charter called it quits after three days because he felt the boat wasn't ready. He went and chartered another boat. I turned the let down into looking at it like a blessing in disguise. I took advantage of the time and worked hard on the boat with the last bit of inspiration I had left. I was at one of the lowest points of my career. The boat needed so much work and the politics of a small marina in a foreign country was beginning to overwhelm me. I had three days until our next charter to get it together, so I dug deep to get the last things done.

I soon found the inspiration I was so desperate for. Our good friend Terry Fohey showed up two days early with his friend Shawn Danke. When I saw the familiar faces I began to feel better. Terry has a glow of power within him, and he has a way of bringing out the best in everyone he comes in contact with. We had caught an 1,188 pound black marlin with him on the *Duyfken* with Peter Wright on our last day of the 1993 season. Coming off such a great trip I told Terry the story of our battle to get the boat dialed-in, and began to prepare him for a week of struggling with the boat when he interrupted me and said, "Don't worry Kev, we'll get 'em."

We didn't waste another minute. We got a few things together and we got out a day early. The three of us left the marina and saw a fish right off the bat. A nice fish, 600 pounds or so, and missed him after three tries. We finished the day with no real problems and I finally felt like we were ready.

We set out our first morning and worked the beautiful coast with the other boats. The fish were still biting and we were in the middle of it but with no action. Scotty said, "Hey Kev, what have we got down there that is big?"

We agreed we needed big lures to get big bites. We went downstairs and found what we thought at the time to be too big, but we put it out anyway. The day wore on and still no bites. I tried to get my feeling of the grounds while Scotty fixed and rigged things on the boat as we fished. I began to wonder what it was going to take to get a bite when I heard all of them laughing uncontrollably downstairs. Scotty was installing something when he felt what he thought was the drill going through the boat. Terry looked up the side to see a 1/4 inch drill bit spinning through the new paint job. Scotty pulled the bit out of the hole, and we were laughing at how funny it was when a bomb went off on the right short. All of sudden all the work we had done and all of the adversity we had faced faded away as fast as the line emptied the reel. After a twenty minute fight we tagged our Madeira fish at 900 pounds with eleven foot four short measurement.

We left the marina the next morning with a different outlook. We had our confidence back and Scotty and I for the first time in months felt like we were there to fish. We did our morning routine, which included cleaning the dirty Racor filters. We headed down the coast to Ribera Brava and our hot lure got covered up by the black spot of an 800 pound fish. After a twenty minute fight the short fat fish that had the head girth of a grander, and the short measurement of a 700 pound fish, swam away with a tag in her back. Now we knew what we were doing there and all of our hopes and dreams were becoming reality.

We fished to the west most of the day and returned to the spot we had caught the fish in the morning. I marked a scratch of bait and looked back to find a monster on Scotty's favorite lure on the long right. At the first sight of the length and girth of the black spot, I yelled down, "It a grander! It's a grander!" The fish sat there windshield wiping and had taken about fifty yards of line when the hook pulled. We told Terry to wind it up without much hope of seeing the fish again. I started a turn to go back through the area when I saw the fish all over the lure again.

Terry wound the lure into position and the enormous black spot came to the lure more aggressive and more committed than the first time. She pushed a big wake off of her forehead and her dorsal stood high out of the water. She focused in and ate the lure from the inside out, laid there for a second and took off. We cleared the other lures and turned and chased like we had on nearly every fish that challenged while fishing with Peter Wright on the Reef. Terry was familiar with the fighting style he had learned from Pete, and we fought the fish like we had so many times together all over the world.

Every time we caught up to the fish and put the pressure on she would go down. I changed the angle every few minutes and Scotty helped Terry manage the drag. We couldn't do anything with the fish and realized early on that the fish had the leader under its belly and we needed to put the heat on it in order to make her stop. We stopped the fish only after we got to seventy pounds of drag. At this point we began to try to get angle and begin to plane the fish. The little boat that needed so much work and had come so far was hooked up to a big fish, and it was doing what we dreamed she would do for us. About twenty minutes of planning went by and we began to get some line. We came back on the angle three times when on the fourth plane the rod tip jumped and all of our hearts stopped. The load on the rod was gone. Was the fish gone? Had we put too much drag on it and ripped the hook out or broken the line? I bumped the throttles ahead and time stood still. After what seemed an hour the load reappeared on the Ian Miller 130. We were still in the game.

Scotty and I agreed that we would back it off a little, knowing that we had rolled the fish out of the tangled leader and that we were now fair hooked in the mouth. We weren't sure how well the fish was hooked so we took our time planning the 200 remaining yards of line. Now the fish came easy due to pulling her up forward not backward. In fifteen minutes we had color. Was the fish as big as we thought? Would the hooks hold? We were soon to find out.

The fish neared the surface and as Scotty reached for the leader I couldn't keep from saying to myself in my mind, "That is a monster! That is a monster!" She popped up alongside with no life in her eyes. Scotty got her up alongside and Shawn and I helped try to revive her as Terry held our twelve foot tag stick next to the fish. Her short measurement was eleven feet eight inches on the pole. Now we had to revive the fish and get her free. After twenty minutes of trying she showed no signs of life. It was only our third fish of the season we really didn't want to bring the fish in. After considering sinking the fish out there with the chance it might come alive, we pulled her in the boat.

We measured her tail at twenty-one inches and her short measurement re-measured eleven feet eight inches. We were sure we had our first grander. We sat there in disbelief. We all had done what we had come to do. We kept shaking each others hand and the smiles shined in the afternoon sun as the boat rocked in the wakes of the other boats coming by to see the fish. Then panic struck.

Terry asked us, "Is there supposed to be water in the front of the boat?" The blood rushed out of my then happy face as it occurred to me that the great fish was now sinking us. I ran to the throttles and Scotty threw open the hatches. At full throttle, full of fishermen, a thousand pound fish and hundreds of gallons of water, we were going max six knots. This would keep us from going down, but for how long? Scotty checked the pumps. Through the fuel and oil that was on the surface of the bilge water he found that the pumps were clogged up with wire tie ends, wire clippings, sawdust, rust and other bits from rebuilding the boat. All the backing down and chasing had washed out the bilge from places we couldn't clean. Once he cleaned the pumps the water flew out the through-hulls and we picked up speed. Once the water was out of the boat we safely made it to shore and weighed the fish at the *French Look*. James Roberts officially weighted the fish in at 1,075.

We were on top of the world and we were going to really get them now. Young and overconfident, we were unbeatable. We had been through a lot, but now it was going to be our time to shine. We were soon to learn that sportfishing was a world full of lessons and that a big lesson was about to present itself to us.

The next morning we left the marina like we were on a victory lap, in good spirits and feeling the six extra Coral beers we had the night before. Now everything was good. We forgot that we almost sank the night before and that we had fuel problems, and that the boat was out of alignment. Everything was great as we set out the lures and headed for the west where the bite had been the day before.

On the way down I saw Barkey Garnsey hooked-up on Stewart Campbell's boat, the *Chunda*. He was hooked-up far to the west. The smoke from the Lugger engines was a sign that they were busy with fish. They had run down there and gotten into them right away. With the experienced and well-run team, Barkey continued to catch one after another. We trolled through the spot where we had our fish the day before and approached them while they fought their fourth fish over 600 pounds. Just as we started to mark the bait, a 700 pound fish bit the short right and we were off to the races. As we backed down on the fish that was now close to the boat, I lost the port engine. It restarted and came back again. Scotty go the leader and I charged back on the fish. As the fish tightened up on Scotty's glove, he told me to come on back because he was feeling the fish making a move on us. I poured it on and we charged back when I lost the port engine again. This time it wouldn't start. The fish gained on Terry and we fought it from a dead boat while we tried to figure out what happened to the motor.

Scotty and I stood in disbelief as we learned that we were out of fuel about as far to the west as we could be in the middle of what was shaping up to be the best bite of the season. We tagged our fish on one motor as the other boats began to troll in and hook up. We sat humiliated watching the boats fight their fish as we tried to figure out what had happened and how we were going to get home. We were going to have a long wait until the boats finished their fishing to tow us in, so we slowly limped away from the bite and headed for home on one engine on the fumes we had left in the tank.

How could this happen? We were supposed to have plenty of fuel to fish two days. With all the work and all of the filter trouble we had, we didn't get the gasket right on the filter and we hadn't noticed that we were leaking fuel. When we opened the engine to full throttle getting our fish in the evening before, we burned a ton of fuel and now we were out. Our feelings of triumph and good fortune were now the last things on our minds. We now were as humbled as we had ever been. The phrase "hero to zero" began to sink in. Our lesson in being even more humble had just begun.

Our good friend Anibal Fernandez, the fine captain of Roddy Hayes's *Lara Jade*, brought us two six gallon jugs of fuel and we gratefully accepted them and started our way home. We got to Ribera Brava and I could see a gas station sign from the sea. I asked

Scotty if he thought we could make it. His answer was no. We were going to have to pray that the gas station had diesel. We went in and took the empty jugs ashore and Terry and Shawn minded the boat. After a half hour we were back with the fuel and we were on the way home. We had learned a great lesson. The class and understanding of Terry, one of my favorite anglers, helped get us through that day.

The rest of that trip went like a fairytale. We caught a bunch more fish and our humble approach to our fishing seemed to work for us. The little boat that barely ran, and that had so many little things wrong with it, taught us valuable lessons that Scotty and I still carry with us today. The memories of the first season are memories that will be with me as long as I fish. It pushed us to limits that I haven't been pushed to since. The first season set the groundwork for the many good times we had in the following four seasons. Things came easier and the fishing rolled.

Looking back, it took a lot of guts to take that responsibility on ourselves and to take the leap of faith to go and challenge the unknown. It was a difficult decision to leave our great jobs and go start something new. We owe our survival of that first season to all the anglers from all over the world that fished on our boat and on boats around us. They all brought their hopes of big fish and faith in our ability. The inspiration that our friends like Terry brought us at the right times gave us the confidence we needed to succeed.

The little underdog boat, the *Pesca Grossa's* humbling beginning, has helped us remember that the inspiration and confidence that you have to have can overcome incredible odds. Once we made it through that first season, we all captains, crews and anglers alike, enjoyed the best of times fishing there in the seasons to come.

I went to fish for the great fish of Madeira and left there with a lot more than I expected. The commitment and desire it took to get to fish there has made the memories of the fishing, the friends and family, and the beautiful culture of the Portuguese island life so strong.

From left to right - mate Digger O'Toole, angler Bill Tweedle, Captain Peter
Wright and mate Kevin Nakamaru on the dock at Blue Water Marina,
Bimini, Bahamas. This blue fin tuna was caught on June 12, 1993
in tuna alley off Cat Cay. It weighted 971 pounds and was the
Bahamas record blue fin at the time.

Captain
Peter Wright

©Kevin Nakamaru

CAPTAIN PETER WRIGHT

Peter Wright grew up in Fort Lauderdale, Florida and began working on charter sport fishing boats out of Hillsboro Inlet while still in grade school. From age eleven through high school he fished on weekends and during summer vacations. He first fished in the Bahamas with noted Pompano Beach Capt. John Whitmer at age eleven and fished many marlin tournaments in Bimini throughout high school and college.

In 1967, Wright visited the Antarctic collecting cephalopods (squid and octopus) as chief scientist for the Univ. of Miami aboard a research cruise of the United States Antarctic Research Program. He traveled throughout the South Pacific upon his return to New Zealand and first fished off the Great Barrier Reef in 1968.

Wright has fished every season in Cairns, Australia since 1968. Besides residing in Australia, Wright owned and operated a charter boat in Kona, Hawaii for five years. He currently resides in Stuart, Florida between fishing adventures.

Among the waters Wright has fished are Australia, New Zealand, New Guinea, Indonesia, Thailand, Mauritius, Kenya, Mozambique, South Africa, The Ivory Coast, Bom Bom Island, Cape Verde Islands, Canary Islands, Madeira, Puerto Rico, Dominican Republic and the Virgin Islands, Bahamas, US Gulf and East Coast, Canada's Maritime Provinces, East and West Coasts of Mexico, Guatamala, Costa Rica, Panama, Ecuador, Chile, Peru, French Polynesia, Fiji, Hawaii and the Galapagos.

As a captain, Wright has caught more marlin over 1,000 pounds than any captain or angler in history and has won dozens of tournaments and guided his clients to numerous records. These include the Australian men's record 1,442 pound Black Marlin on 130 pound line, women's eighty pound class World and Australian record of 1323 pounds. He holds the Bahamas Bluefin Tuna record of 972 pounds and guided angler Stewart Campbell to a single day's record of seventy-three Giant Bluefin Tuna tagged and released off Cape Hatteras, N.C.

As a contributing editor, Wright wrote the Sportfishing column for Motor Boating and Sailing along with many feature articles and boat reports for over thirteen years. He was consultant editor for Blue Water Magazine. He gives seminars and consults in the marine and electronics industries and for major fishing tackle companies and is on the Pro Staff for Bass Pro Shops and Offshore Angler.

Captain Wright is Editor at Large for World Publications where he writes a big game fishing column for Marlin Magazine and also feature articles for Sportfishing and Marlin. He also hosts television shows and conducts seminars and "Marlin University" programs.

He continues to fish Australia's Great Barrier Reef every October and November.

A MARLIN TO REMEMBER
by
PETER WRIGHT

You always remember your biggest marlin but others stick in your mind for different reasons. A black marlin that we tagged and released one day in the middle of Australia's Cormorant Pass that then turned on a dime and crashed into the boat and skewered my deckhand in the chest with its massive bill is burned into my brain. I could never forget that fish. Those of you who saw professionally distributed copies of the home video that was shot that day probably won't forget either, and many of you have questioned me about the day Jimmy Burns got speared.

My team on board *Kingfish* included angler Bill Chapman and wireman "Mutt" Coble. I had talked another captain, Jim Burns, into coming along as our third crewman for a couple of weeks. A brick layer by trade, Jim was a handsome young man with a beautiful wife and two small children. He had a great physique with a sculptured musculature he had acquired while lifting thousands of bricks and concrete blocks.

Joining us on the first mother ship trip to ever go this far north of Cairns were noted Australian Captain Peter Bristow and his crew and charter on *Avalon*. Along with our catamaran mother ship the *Tropic Queen* we trolled north along the outside edge of the Great Barrier Reef and when we were due east of Lizard Island we reached the top of Number Ten Ribbon Reef.

We had wonderful fishing as we progressed farther and farther north, but wondered each day when we were going to get too far up the reef and run out of fish. Some days one or the other game boat would have slow fishing but the other would have a great day and we kept pressing on into new territory.

I couldn't believe my eyes the morning I saw a sleek sport fishing cruiser approaching from the north. Garrick Agnew, an Australian multimillionaire, had heard about the giant marlin being caught off Cairns and had run his custom built fifty-three foot *Pannawonica* completely around the top half of Australia, over three thousand miles from their home port of Perth. On *Kingfish* we had already tagged two or three marlin that day and just before the two boats met in the middle of Cormorant Pass, we hooked up again.

The fish made a long run with enormous greyhounding leaps across the surface. Anywhere else in the world a 600 pound marlin would have been a trophy. Here it was above average, but no where near "large", and well short of the "it's a horse" distinction we used for marlin over 1,000 pounds and later called "granders".

The hook might have started out in the fish's mouth, or maybe it was hooked in the fish's back from the start. In either case the marlin rapidly got line off the big Fin Nor reel faster than I could back up in *Kingfish*. It took 200 yards out before I could get the boat turned around and give chase.

I ran *Kingfish* at planing speed from the control station in the tower. As we chased the marlin across the waves I could see the remains of the scad bait lying on its shoulder, where the hook had caught near the dorsal fin.

Chapman had recovered most of the line by the time the marlin began to slow down to try to recover from the oxygen debt incurred in the long sustained run. All those majestic leaps had helped burn up the oxygen available in the blood stream, and oxygen was necessary to allow the mighty muscles to function.

The thought flashed through my mind that here was our chance to show the new guys how a really good crew fought and caught marlin. I dropped from the tower to the flying bridge and spun *Kingfish* with the engines to allow us to back up after the marlin. Because I had stopped in a position upsea and upwind from the fish, I was able to back up FAST with no water pouring over the transom covering boards and little spray even reaching the angler and crew.

The marlin continued to swim down sea and came to the surface in order to surf on the swell and chop generated by days of fifteen to twenty-five knot southeast trade winds. As the fish got a free ride from each wave, the tip of its huge sickle tail would protrude slightly above the surface of the water and, through our polarized sun glasses, we could all see the color of the huge body under the surface.

I kept *Kingfish* backing up hard but angled her off to one side. When he had two turns of the thirty feet of doubled 130 pound line safely around the reel, Chapman increased the drag. With the boat racing back after the fish, and the increased drag slowing the marlin's forward speed, we continued to gain line until the big snap swivel connecting line and leader came within Mutt's reach.

Mutt, a tall, burly, and athletic man took hold of the swivel and heaved, then got a wrap of wire around a gloved hand and heaved again. The fish came ever closer to the boat. Now I could see that the leader was tangled around the fish and was pulling from a point behind the rigid bone of the pectoral fins. The marlin was both hooked in the dorsal fin and lassoed by a hitch of wire around its body. Mutt would not be able to lead the fish from the head as one does a horse by its reins. He would be trying to pull the twelve foot long, 600 pound body sideways through the water.

The black marlin and the boat were both racing down sea with the fish alongside and to starboard. It was swimming parallel to the cockpit, with its head even with our transom, when Jim stepped in for the tag shot. As he reached out with the ten foot tag pole the marlin spurted forward past our stern and hurled itself into the air - out of his reach.

"Don't break it!" I yelled from the bridge as the marlin launched itself into the air again. Mutt bent his knees to keep his body low so he could pull against the steel wire with his full strength. The marlin's leap went up more than out and Mutt, gauging the strain on the wire, continued to hold on. As the marlin went airborne in a high reverse somersault, Jim scuttled around Mutt to reach out over the stern to apply the tag. I rapidly shifted from reverse to forward, then applied full throttle.

"Watch your hands!" I cried as water from the spinning props jetted out from under the stern and first stopped our reverse momentum, then started accelerating *Kingfish* forward. The boat was starting to move away from the fish but, although I didn't know it yet, Mutt's thickly gloved hands were not our greatest concern.

Jim reached far out over the transom and tagged the marlin in the shoulder as it finished the somersault and landed on its side with a huge splash. The video camera shows Jim backing up to get away from the marlin as it instantly jumped again -but this time directly toward the boat.

I remember the boat starting to move, but too slowly. The video shows Jim getting caught by the armrest of the chair and being unable to move away from the oncoming fish as it came over the covering board and half into the boat. In the video you can see the bill making contact with Jim's left side and some people claim to see a bulge in the back of his shirt in one frame.

I heard a cry that registered at the time as "got him" as the fish landed half on the covering board and fell back into the sea. I thought the crew meant the tag was in, and we didn't need to continue with the fish. The boat sped away from the tagged marlin and Mutt hung on and broke the wire. Then I saw Jim clutch his chest, sit on the starboard gunwale, and stagger into the salon and out of my sight.

I stuffed the gear levers into the neutral position and leapt from the bridge into the cockpit. I was the first one to reach Jim who sat on the salon floor, leaning against the port-side day bed. He was holding his chest, slightly to the left of center, directly above where most people think the heart lies. Blood stained his shirt and oozed through his fingers.

My heart sank and I thought to myself, "Oh God, I talked him into coming with us and now I've killed him - and his family, what'll they do? I've done it this time!"

I remember feeling terribly melodramatic as I grabbed his collared polo shirt and ripped it open. I was expecting a huge hole right in the center of his chest and when I saw a smaller wound, over to one side, closer to his armpit, I felt a rush of relief.

The relief was short lived when I realized that the tissue I could see protruding through the lips of the wound was part of Jim's lung that had been pulled out when the rasp-like bill had exited after penetrating his upper body. I grabbed half of the torn shirt and wadded it up to hold it over the wound.

"Get me something to make a bandage." I said over my shoulder to the others who stood behind me. "No, not the paper towels, get a clean sheet and tear it in strips. Quick!"

We made a bandage of a folded section of sheet secured with strips of sheet tied around his chest and made Jim as comfortable as we could. He sat on the salon floor leaning back against a corner formed by the day berth and the bulkhead. "Let him rinse his mouth with water." I said to the others. "But don't drink anything Jim. We're heading for Lizard Island. You're going to be all right."

The Viet Nam War was still in full swing with guys suffering horrible chest wounds every day and I figured that if we could get Jim to a hospital quickly enough he would be OK. Briefly, I thought about the risk of infection from the material that could have been introduced by the bill, but reasoned that if Jim lived long enough to have an infection, with modern antibiotics, his chances of coming through this were excellent.

I grabbed a chart and ran up into the tower. There was no LORAN or GPS in Australia in those days, and no buoys or aids to navigation in these remote waters, but a glance at the chart showed a narrow pass through the outer reef, then several miles of open water without having to worry about coral heads. I grabbed the radio and called a May Day, which was answered immediately, as I throttled up and started to run for help.

Within minutes I had relayed our situation to Bob Dyer who was fishing much farther south on his Bertram *Tennessee II*. I planned to head for Lizard Island and asked that the Royal Flying Doctor Service send one of their airplanes to the small dirt landing strip that I had been told existed on the uninhabited island. Confirmation of my message and the successful relay to shore by boats nearer to Cairns brightened the outlook.

I stopped in the calmer, more protected, water inside the reef and went below to check on Jim. I unwrapped the blood soaked bandages in order to reappraise the damage and relay it to the doctors. Jim tried to sit up and blood poured from the hole in his chest. He fell back against the bunk. I was sure that what I could see was lung tissue, but Jim's pulse remained strong and he was conscious, alert, and very deliberately breathing slowly and steadily. I reapplied the bandages.

"I got through to Bob Dyer and he relayed it to Cairns. The flying doctor has been contacted." I tried to reassure my friend.

"Try to stay comfortable. We're going to get you to a hospital. You're going to be OK." I tried to be more optimistic than I felt and didn't say anything about the punctured lung.

Bill Chapman came into the tower with me and held the chart open in the wind so I could see how to approach the island. "It didn't look too bad." he said quietly.

"Bill, I could see lung tissue and he may be bleeding badly internally. We have to get him to a hospital. If he can live that long I think he'll be OK. If he dies before that there's nothing else we can do."

I had decided to run the boat up onto the beach if necessary, but we found a small commercial fishing boat in the anchorage and they lent us a dinghy.

We moved Jim off the deck and onto the bunk once we anchored in the calm waters of the lagoon. After talking to him and again checking his pulse, I went ashore and found a caretaker, the sole inhabitant of the lovely island, living in a tent on the beach front site where a fancy new resort that would become today's Lizard Island Lodge was soon to be built.

The caretaker's radio had the flying doctor frequency and soon I was talking to a Doctor who was already in the air aboard their air ambulance. They would be able to land at Lizard Island in under an hour. "Take off the bandage and make an airtight covering over the wound. We want to prevent his lung from collapsing if it hasn't already. Plastic cling wrap under a bandage will do," came through a background of static. "Move him ashore, off the boat, we can do surgery on the spot if necessary."

We decided not to follow these instructions. The inside layers of sheet were soaked with blood and I was sure our bandage was already airtight. The boat was cleaner than any place on the island and it was completely still in the anchorage in the island's lee. If there was emergency surgery to be done we would let the doctor decide if the island was better than the boat.

We waited alongside the dirt strip with a small tractor. When the plane landed we carried a doctor and nurse with two large wooden cases and a stretcher to the beach and ferried them and their equipment to *Kingfish.*

Quickly and efficiently the team sprang into action. The wooden boxes unfolded into an emergency operating theater complete with instruments and oxygen. They could have done open chest surgery on the spot and my relief at no longer being in charge was enormous! Less than two hours had elapsed since the accident.

After an inspection that revealed a partially collapsed lung, we strapped Jim onto a stretcher and transported him by boat and tractor back to the waiting airplane. After take off the plane flew at almost zero altitude, skimming the waves en route to Cairns. A decrease in atmospheric pressure from a high flying airplane could be fatal.

The pitch dark of a moonless tropical night caught us several miles short of our mother ship. I picked my way slowly through the treacherous coral heads with the the the aid of a spotlight. When we finally reached safety at *Tropic Queen* they yelled across the water that the evening news on the radio had reported Jim Burns was resting comfortably in Cairns Base Hospital in "good" condition. Our ordeal was over.

Post Script:

Within two weeks Jim was back at sea running a boat. When we got a chance to talk I told him I had not wanted him to know how serious I believed his injuries to be as we ran for help. He in turn had thought we did not appreciate how badly he was hurt.

"I had this feeling that if I could keep from coughing and tearing myself up I might make it." he said. "The urge to cough was awful but I tried to keep breathing steadily."

The doctors told Jim that the punctured lung was serious, but even more importantly, the tip of the bill had only missed his heart by millimeters. His heavily muscled chest had made the difference in the fraction of an inch that was in turn the difference between life and death in our encounter with a marlin that none of us who were there will ever forget.

Every year I send a donation to the Royal Flying Doctor Service!

Captain
Bouncer Smith

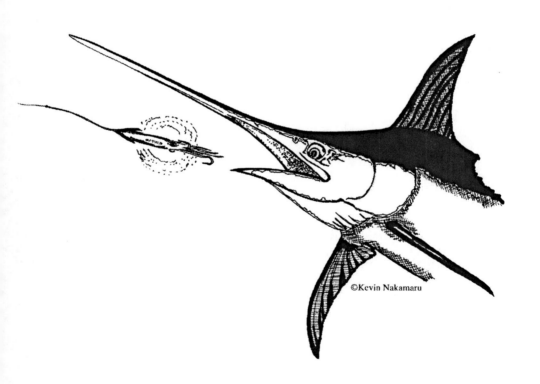

©Kevin Nakamaru

CAPTAIN BOUNCER SMITH

Bouncer Smith started his fishing at the age of five in Pontiac, Michigan with bluegills from the shore of Square Lake. He was making the outdoor report headline in the newspaper with a couple two pound trout at seven years of age. He rigged his own double hooked ballyhoo and caught a sailfish on it when he was eight.

After moving to Miami he worked as bait assistant and live bait salesman on Sunny Isles Pier. He was thirteen at the time. Bouncer's first party boat job was New Years Eve, 1963, on board the *Mucho K* out of Haulover Park in Miami. Upon graduation from high school in 1966 he worked as first mate nights on the *Sea Breeze* out of the famous Pier Five. By September, 1966, he worked nights on *Sea Breeze*, and during the day he mated on the *Sea Gull Jr.*, a charter boat. He worked from 7 AM till 1:30 AM. In 1967 he returned to Haulover aboard *Popeye* at night, and onboard charter boat *Duchess* during the day. Then in that fall he moved to Castaway Docks to work aboard charter boat *Bandit*.

Bouncer received his Captain's License on March 13, 1968 and started running the *Bandit* on March 14th. June 1st of that year he moved to the charter boat *Top Luck* and began fishing marlin in the Bahamas as mate and part time captain.

From 1973 to March of 1976 Captain Smith fished out of Bahia Mar in Fort Lauderdale aboard *Doctor's Orders* and many say he introduced kite fishing to Broward County.

On March 1, 1976 Bouncer went into business for himself at Bud and Mary's in Islamorada in the Florida Keys. Flats fishing was a high school dream he had to live. He spent two seasons (March through June and November through June) there, and fished Ocean

City, Maryland in the summers (July through September). This was canyon fishing for white marlin and yellowfin tuna.

Bouncer returned to Miami in the fall of 1977 and ran a party boat and guided on the Miami area flats, and taught people how to fish their own boats. In 1979, he moved up to a twenty foot skiff and found his place in the fishing world. Bouncer has been a sailfish and tarpon guide ever since.

Buying his first Dusky in 1981 put him where he is today. He continued to visit Ocean City through 1981, but soon built his skiff guiding business to 300 trips a year.

In 1997 Bouncer Won the Hyman Award from the Met Fishing Tournament and Miami Beach Rod and Reel Club "Guide of the Year".

In 1999 he won The Billfish Foundation "Captain of the Year". That was the same year he achieved a world record for halibut on fly (111 Pounds).

In 2002 he won the Miami Billfish Tournament "Bob Lewis Memorial" Public Service Award. In his career Bouncer has guided anglers to over fifty world records and has won numerous local and international tournaments.

Bouncer is active in Make-a-Wish and other youth activities and was the Co-Founder of South Florida Fishing Club, and is a member of several other fishing clubs. He is on the Board of Directors of Yamaha/Contender Miami Billfish Tournament.

Today he is a charter captain on his own boat, *Bouncer's Dusky 33*, out of Miami Beach Marina.

MY GREATEST FISHING ADVENTURE

by

BOUNCER SMITH

It was October, 2002. Dr. Marty Arostegui had talked about trying for a swordfish on fly for over a year. We had caught swordfish with the fly rod on board, but we never made a cast with it. The full moon had been four nights earlier. We had learned over the years that swordfish usually feed closer to the surface when the moon was not above the horizon. The moon rises four hours after sunset four nights after the full moon. This allowed Marty three hours of fly fishing before the moon rise and after it was fully dark. It also allowed him to fish during a 'minor solunar feeding period' at the time of moonrise.

We ran Marty's thirty-five foot Cabo to an area known as the Triple Lumps off Key Biscayne on this perfect swordfish night. The ocean was flat calm. To increase the odds of catching something, I put a rigged squid on a fifty pound outfit, lowered the bait to 100 feet and added a float. This bait was floated out 200 feet from the boat. A second rod was baited with a live blue runner and lowered to 200 feet. A float was added to this line and set out 100 feet from the boat.

In my opinion the next move was very important. I lowered a Hydro Glow fish light into the water, next to the boat. The Hydro Glow cast an eerie green glow for about 100 feet all around the boat. Soon baitfish and small predator fish gathered in the light.

While all this took place, Marty prepared his tackle. He selected a large two hook fly he had tied for halibut fishing in Alaska. He secured this to an eighty pound shock leader that was

163

spliced to a twenty pound class tippet. He chose a 450 grain sinking fly line on a large arbor Gulfstream fly reel and twelve weight rod. As he prepared to cast, I provided Marty with a "Lunker Light", a miniature cyalume light stick. This was attached between the hooks of the fly. Now Marty's fly lit up like some kind of deep water sea creature. Marty stationed himself in the stern of the drifting boat and began to cast. As he cast, let the fly and line sink and then slowly worked it back to the boat, I told sea stories to his son Martini.

Marty had been casting and retrieving for about half an hour when his fly suddenly stopped. His rod jerked violently once, and then again. Line ripped through Marty's fingers and just as suddenly the line went limp. He retrieved his fly with no apparent damage. I thought about all the fish that could have been on the fly. The ocean was full of life. Baitfish, small predators and who knows how many different kinds of bigger predators could have struck Marty's fly?

Another hour passed. Martini fell asleep. Marty and I talked of how low the odds were of catching a swordfish on fly. We knew that a fly fishing angler had caught a couple off SE Africa by raising the fish to slow trolled lures at night. We knew one man had caught a six pound swordfish in the Mediterranean Sea while casting for bonitos during the day. We could catch one, but how many years could it take? We had not even had a bite on our two proven swordfish baits.

Marty's fly rod jerked toward the water! Line screamed from his reel! A fast fish had grabbed his fly and headed toward Bermuda. I hollered for Martini to wake up, wound in the nearest fifty pound outfit and raced to clear it so we could take off in pursuit of Marty's unidentified adversary. As soon as I had cleared that one line I raced to the helm. Before I could touch the controls, Marty called out that the fish had stopped or turned. Marty was gaining line. Over and over I tried to wake Martini while I watched the progress that his father made at bringing his foe within the circle of light provided by the Hydro Glow.

I knew Marty was hooked to a big skipjack tuna, barracuda, jack or shark. There was no way it could be a swordfish on fly only ninety minutes into a long-shot adventure. The battle went on for about thirty minutes. There were short runs, followed by slow gains typical of direct drive fly reels. The odds of this fish being a swordfish or shark went up as time went by. Lesser fish would have arrived at the boat by now. Could it be the swordfish we were hunting?

"It's got a bill!" was heard all over the western Atlantic as I hollered my excitement when the fish swam into the lighted area around the boat. I soon pulled a forty-six inch swordfish into the boat. Too many photos were taken as this beautiful fish held it's breath. We put our foe back into the sea as a warm feeling of victory rose through both angler and captain. Marty had succeeded in angling's greatest accomplishment. He had rigged his own rod, tied his own fly and all the knots. He cast and worked his own creation well enough to entice a great game fish to eat it. And then he had fought one of the ocean's greatest gladiators to the boat with no help from the maneuvering of the boat. One great man verses one great fish. Poor Martini slept through the whole battle. He woke up about ten minutes after we released the fish. The good news for Martini was that about twenty minutes after he woke up, a swordfish ate the squid that was still out there on a fifty pound outfit. A twin to the fish that ate the fly was soon released. We hope it will grow into a spawning adult in a couple years. Swordfish have been documented to grow from thirty to 120 pounds in two years.

I only called about thirty people between midnight and eight in the morning to tell them what I had been witness to, that beautiful night, with a master fly fisherman. We have learned of another swordfish caught on fly since that evening. This was another nine or ten pound fish caught off New Jersey while targeting tuna at night. Still it is quite an honor to be there when someone joins a world wide union of only four or five.

TARPON

by

BOUNCER SMITH

At Montana State University, Bozeman, where my son Terry was going to school in 2000, the dormitory was full of young men from the Rocky Mountain States. These fellows worshiped their trout and they would come in every week with tales of rainbows and brown trout that were fifteen and eighteen and even twenty-three inches long . Over this particular Thanksgiving break Terry decided to stay out West while many of his friends headed to the streams to participate in their trout fishing rituals. One day right after school resumed, Terry called me on the phone to share in a desire he had developed. On Christmas break he needed to catch and photograph a big tarpon. This was something, the magnitude of which, his pals could never comprehend.

When Terry returned for the Christmas break we set out in search of that good sized tarpon. Now by tarpon standards we're only talking good sized, not giant. I'm talking about a 120 pound beauty, just what Terry had hoped for, and it was hooked up in our first hour out. It was a strong and very active jumper but Terry whipped it in short order. When a tarpon is totally tired out it will lay on the surface and barely move. Terry grabbed the fish by the lower jaw and lifted the head slightly off the surface of the water. I was positioned just behind the tail. The camera captured the whole fish from its tail to its massive head, and Terry's huge grin. We had that four by six picture laminated so Terry could keep it in his pocket. Back at MSU, every time someone started bragging about their trout, Terry was quick to show them what a real big fish looked like.

* * * * * * * * * * * * * * * * *

We parked on the side of the dirt road on the edge of this industrial area. We were directly under some huge power lines. Jack and Craig led the way through the light, waist-high vegetation while discussing how to escape the imminent attack of one of the huge alligators known to live in this swampy area. Craig said it would be easy. "He was faster than Jack or me!" After a couple hundred yards we came to a dirt road with water filled ditches down each side. The far side of each ditch was lined with thick mangrove trees.

As Jack had instructed, I was ready with a four pound spinning outfit rigged with a twenty-pound monofilament leader and a 'double O' Reflecto spoon. We spread out and started casting. Fish were lazily rolling on the surface and soon one crashed my spoon. It struck with a vengeance! My quarry, the mighty silver king, flew through the air and slammed down on the dirt road. Blood flowed from his gills, he never moved a muscle. I picked him up out of the road and studied him. He looked exactly like his full grown relatives, big scales, tough bony upturned jaws, chrome colored sides with a dark back and a long streamer off the trailing edge of his dorsal fin. He still sits on my book shelf sealed in epoxy resin.

This juvenile tarpon had come to the now mostly developed Port Everglades as a worm-like larvae. Thriving on the millions of mosquito larvae that lived in these mangrove swamps, he should have been safe to grow to ten or fifteen pounds before taking on the open water world. An over-excited big game fishing guide had shortened his life by fifty years or more. He may have reached close to 100 pounds, and if he was really a she, it could have been her that would have set a new world record a year or two ago of 290 pounds.

The ditches are still there, but with "Homeland Security" in place, no young angler visits them. I hope the tarpon still grow up there.

Tarpon are my "ultimate game fish." You can hunt them by size. You can use bait, lure or fly. They can drive you crazy when they are off their feed. They fight hard and jump high. You can pick your scenery from fresh water residential canals, everglades swamp, open bay or coastal beaches. On top of all that, we never kill one, making it a very clean sport.

My chosen hunting ground for tarpon is Miami, Florida. I fish for the silver king along the beaches of Miami Beach from November to July. The tarpon are like the 'snow birds'. They come down when it gets too cold up north and go back when it gets too hot down here. It must be something in the water, tarpon and snow birds attempt to reproduce while they are here.

When we target tarpon along the beach, we generally use twenty pound conventional outfits with lever drags. We splice on a twelve foot leader of fifty pound monofilament using a Yucatan knot and then add two or three feet of eighty-pound mono at the end.

Shrimp are the first choice of bait from November through March. With this bait we use a 3/0 to 5/0 "J" hook like the Eagle Claw L194. This is snelled to the end of the leader. The hook is passed crossways through the cheeks of the shrimp. Let one out about 120 feet, add another about eighty feet from the boat and you are ready for action. Fish your lever drag reels with the drag at about three pounds. It is best to let Mr. Rod Holder hook your fish, but if you prefer to hold on to your rod yourself, then do nothing when you feel a strike. The tarpon will roll up on your shrimp, close its mouth and turn to swim down and back to its station. The hook will catch in the upper lip and the fight will be on. Keep your rod high during those runs, and point your rod at the fish when he goes airborne. This will reduce the pressure on the hook when the fish accelerates and throws her head from side to side while flying through the air. With any breeze at all, you may want to add a rig to your spread with a split shot sinker or a ¼ or 3/8 ounce "Hook Up." With the weighted hook, you will hook the shrimp up through the head, instead of crossways.

Once the fish has burned off some energy, push that drag up to four or five pounds and let the battle begin. When dealing with tarpon, you can finish the fight quick or it can go on for hours. If you drive along next to the fish and never try to stop its forward motion, it will swim for hours. If you apply pressure against the fish's forward motion, it will burn out quickly. Pull your rod down and opposite the direction of the fish whenever possible.

From April through all of June, crabs are usually the bait of choice. Shrimp still work if you can get them that are large enough to carry your hook. The crabs should be about one to three inches across the shell.

For wild strikes, but less solid hook ups, slow troll live mullet in the fall and spring. The show is great and you'll catch more than enough fish. Pinfish always produce a few strikes as will any small bottom fish. With the small bottom fish and crabs, a float may be necessary to keep your rig from hanging bottom when the drift is slow.

For your plug rod or spinning outfit, try mirror lures, Tsumani rubber baits, DOA lures and bucktails for casting. In March there are nights when you can hear tarpon crashing shrimp all around the boat. They hit surface lures better than drifted live baits.

On calm days, if boat traffic is light, you may find tarpon suspended on the surface at the end of their roll. These fish are a dream come true for fly casters. On other days, the fish will eat flies if you work hard with a sinking line. Our best tarpon on fly was about 140 pounds.

*   *   *   *   *   *   *   *   *   *   *   *

Ray was doing a good job of that on a memorable Saturday night. He came down from the Northeast a few times every winter. He loved his tarpon fishing. Every time he fished with me, his grandmother, whom he stayed with while in town, would ask when he got home, "Did you catch anything we can eat?"

Ray always had the same answer. "We caught some beautiful tarpon Grams, but no eating fish."

Ray brought Grams and his girlfriend this June evening. The first spot we tried produced no action, but was calm on this breezy afternoon. As the sun went down, the wind went down with it. We decided to try the ocean off Fisher Island. Upon arriving near the end of the jetty, we fired out two live crabs on 8/0 circle hooks. Within seconds we were hooked up. The tarpon jumped in the waning light once, and again, and a third time. The fish flew high in the air within fifty feet of the boat. As we passed the end of the jetty, headed for forty-five feet of water and a long down and dirty fight, the leader reached the rod tip. The fish was a technical catch and Ray swung the tip of the rod to my waiting hand. I grabbed the leader and Ray hollered, "Release him!" I took a turn on the leader and it snapped as we intended. Ray turned to Grams and ask if she had seen the beautiful fish. She never saw it. We had released the fish quickly, because when the fish get in the deep water of the ship channel, the fight can be long and deep, and the fish had already shown his best.

The show was repeated only minutes later. Three or four jumps and a race for the jetty. Another good release and another inquiry of Grams. Again she failed to see the jumps. Ray was thrilled to try again and his girlfriend again turned down an opportunity to take the rod. By now it was pitch dark. It only took a couple minutes to hook-up again. This fish was different. She swam to the jetty and then west along the shallow side of the rocks. This tarpon swam into gin clear water only eight to ten feet deep. I followed with the boat while Ray kept maximum pressure on the rod and fish, and his girlfriend stood in the back of the boat with a camera to her eye, waiting for a photo opportunity. Grams watched from the stern facing seat.

The fish lunged forward and down. You could see it roll under in the clear water, the spotlight reflecting off its side. It raced to the surface, cleared the water and the side of the boat. It crashed down on our camera girl's shoulder and head, and then slammed down on the deck. There was mass hysteria as the fish thrashed, the girls screamed, Ray roared, and I tried to shout orders to keep everyone safe.

I reached over the seat and grabbed Grams under the arms and lifted her around the seat. This put the bench seat between her and the raging fish. Girlfriend was sitting on the fish box with her legs and feet hugged against her chest. Ray stood next to his grandmother. The fish settled down as it starved for oxygen.

I cautiously approached the beaten tarpon. I grabbed it by the lower jaw and wrestled it over the side and into the water. It struggled to swim away in the shallow water.

I moved a shaken Ray's girlfriend to the bow seat. Then I moved Grams up with her and cleaned up the bulk of the blood, slime and whatever else the tarpon had left aboard. I collected about thirty scales for Ray and me to dry out as souvenirs.

When the boat was reasonably clean we moved the girls back to the rear seat and made sure they were not injured. Ray ask Grams, "I guess you saw that fish?" Grams replied powerfully, "Sonny I never want to see your fish again."

JERKS CAN'T USE CIRCLE HOOKS

by

BOUNCER SMITH

Back in the early 80's, I used to fish with Michael every week. All we targeted was tarpon. We wanted to be the kings of tarpon releases in the winter fishing tournament. We fished live shrimp all winter and did well. In the spring, when the mullet ran, we had bad luck. We would loose sixty or seventy percent of the tarpon that ate our live mullet. I switched to 9/0 or 10/0 circle hooks. Michael said to switch back to J hooks after we learned that with the circle hooks, the only way to loose a fish was by breaking the line. Michael said it was too easy to catch the fish that way. We won the tournament for six straight years.

We jump ahead to the 90's. Tim Choates brought Captain Ron Hamlin to the Rod and Reel Club of Miami Beach. They spoke about using only Eagle Claw circle hooks aboard the boats in Guatemala. Captain Ron had declared his boat 'circle hooks or no hooks'.

Well, I reasoned, with all the fish they have down there, they could afford to miss some and still have a good day. They talked about the high mortality of fish caught on J hooks. This got me thinking about how many of our sailfish swam away pumping blood from their gills. Were we kidding ourselves with self righteous release ethics?

I decided to try fishing with circle hooks. My first unsuspecting victims were a father and son, on the boy's first offshore adventure. A double header of sailfish ate the baits early in the trip. Both got away, and all the circle hooks got thrown away immediately. The trip ended well. The boy caught sails, dolphin, kings and a tarpon. His catch gave him the honor of a Gold Coast Grand Slam. That is a sailfish, tarpon and dolphin all in one trip.

The circle hooks were gone from the boat for months. Then I learned that the 5/0 circle hooks I had used were too small to fit around a sailfish jaw, and were headed for failure before we started. Ten months later, I picked my next victim in the circle hook farce. The sailfish were red hot. I was returning from the boatyard and calling anyone who may be able to get out of the office and go fishing. Sue Cocking from the Miami Herald could get away to catch some sailfish. I rigged half the rods with 7/0 circle hooks and half with 5/0 J hooks. We fished for about five hours and caught seven sailfish. We caught four sails on four strikes on the circle hooks. We caught three sails out of four strikes on the J hooks. The lost fish broke the line. It was obvious that circle hooks must be better. After that afternoon adventure, I started using some circle hooks. We would catch five or six on the circle hooks and then lose one. Immediately it would be back to J hooks. I wasn't about to let these silly circle hooks cost me sailfish catches. Catch eight or nine on the circle hooks, lose one and back to J's. The cycle went like that 'til one day when we lost two sails in a row on the circle hooks. We switched back to the J's even though my one and only angler for the day had already released seven sailfish on the circle hooks before those two loses.

The next strike was a small white marlin. It fought and jumped for all it was worth. When we got it to the boat, I grabbed the mono leader. When I pulled on the leader, I could feel the J hook tearing through the insides of the fish. Immediately blood poured from this little white marlin's gills. I released him and he sank away, even as my heart sank inside me knowing we had killed that little guy because we lacked the confidence to fish with the circle hooks.

Eagle Claw hook company should celebrate that day. I have been a crusader for Eagle Claw circle hooks ever since. We now have learned to use Eagle Claw circle hooks for everything. They stay hooked in a fish better than J hooks. Beginning anglers can hook a higher percentage of their strikes with circle hooks. The circle hooks hang bottom less when targeting snook or grouper. And even if you gut hook a fish, the damage to the fish is far less than with J hooks.

A good friend of mine fished a tournament requiring circle hooks last spring and caught every fish that ate his bait. He won that event with five sailfish. The next tournament he fished, he could fish whatever hook he wanted to. He chose J hooks and lost seven out of ten. He should stick with the circle hooks so he could win more tournaments and have fish left out there for when his three year old son grows up and wants to catch some fish. The last tournament we won was captain's choice for hooks. My mate was thrilled that we caught every sail that bit, but was shocked when he learned that we could have used J hooks and didn't.

Using circle hooks require some adjustments to your fishing. First you can not hide the hook in the bait. Second you must size your hook by fish jaw size instead of bait size. And most important, you cannot jerk to hook the fish. The fish must swim away, thus pulling the hook around the corner of it's jaw.

Do your part to maximize the future of fishing by using circle hooks. You can catch more fish while doing it.

Captain Bouncer Smith poses with one of the many swordfish he has caught off the South Florida coast. The largest swordfish ever taken on fly was caught and released by Dr. Marty Arostegui in October 2002. Bouncer Smith was the captain for that adventure.

Captain
"Skip" Smith

©Kevin Nakamaru

CAPTAIN "SKIP" SMITH

Skip Smith began his career in fishing in the early 1960's working on his Dad's drift boat. In the 1970's he then moved on to working on various charter boats and as a long-line commercial fisherman. In 1980 he took over as captain of the fifty-three foot Hatteras and soon to be sixty foot Hatteras, *The Hooker* where he cruised around the east coast of the U.S., the Caribbean, Bahamas and the east and west coast of Panama. In his capacity as captain he was responsible for day-to-day operations of the vessel including running the boat, maintaining it and preparing it for trips offshore. In the mid-1980's he supervised construction of the forty-eight foot G&S *The Hooker,* and was its captain for a six year period. In the later 1980's he supervised a major refit on the world famous 110 foot mothership *The Madam* which piggybacked the forty-eight foot G&S sportfisher *The Hooker.* Skip subsequently captained the vessels and had overall responsibility for trans-Atlantic and trans-Pacific crossings. In that capacity he also secured major sponsors for fishing adventures.

From 1990 to 1995 Skip supervised construction of, and was the captain for the forty-eight foot G&S sport-fisherman *The Sound Machine* where he had overall responsibility for day-to-day operations, maintenance and fishing operations. *The Sound Machine* fished between Florida, the Bahamas, USVI, Venezuela and Panama during those years.

As a Captain, Skip Smith has navigated the waters of the west coast of Central & South America down to Peru and up to Cabo San Lucas, Mexico, as well as the Caribbean waters of Panama, Venezuela, the BVI, the USVI, St. Martin, Guadeloupe, Martinique, Aruba, Dominican Republic, Puerto Rico and Cuba. He also traveled as far east and west to include Hawaii, Tahiti, New Zealand, Australia, South Africa, Senegal, Ivory Coast and the Cape Verde Islands. He holds the USCG one hundred ton Ocean Master license, was responsible for forty-eight IGFA world records, participates on many fishing tournament committees, and is a free lance writer for many fishing and boating magazines.

Since 1991 Skip has been involved in the marine insurance business and is the owner of Merritt-Smith Insurance, Inc. of Pompano Beach, Florida where he handles insurance for yachts, boatyards & marinas. Skip lives in Lighthouse Point, Florida with his wife and three children.

SO MANY FIRSTS
by
SKIP SMITH

There were a lot of firsts. We caught the first Atlantic blue marlin on four pound line, Pacific sail on eight pound tippet, swordfish on four pound line, on and on it goes. We developed and refined the bait and switch. We caught black marlin over 1,000 pounds and thousands of black and blue marlin, white marlin, striped marlin, Atlantic and Pacific sailfish and spearfish. Put them tail to tail and I will take a swordfish any day! One of the reasons why is because when you're trolling, most of the time you get to see the bite and you know what kind of fish you are fighting. When drifting or slow trolling deep for swordfish, you don't know what kind of fish it is, much less the size, until you get the fish close to the boat. You also get to face the nearest animal to a dinosaur. They not only have a bill that could behead you, they attack the boat when you get them close!

My two favorite stories of my career are both with swordfish. Not only did we set six world records during these two trips, we caught numerous other swordfish and lost some real nice ones. (Five records are still standing and the other one was one of our own records that we broke during the second trip).

The Hooker was finished in June of 1985. It was a forty-eight foot G&S built with one purpose in mind, to catch billfish all over the Atlantic and Pacific Oceans and the Caribbean Sea. We started off in the US Virgin Islands, and within the first week of blue marlin fishing, we had one blue marlin of about 500 pounds jump at the boat and impale its bill through the hull right above the water line. OUCH! What a way to break in a new boat. From there we went to Grenada, Venezuela, and then off to the Panama Canal and to Tropic Star Lodge.

We had been fishing for black marlin in Panama every morning, and then off for sailfish in the afternoon for the month of January. Fishing was good as usual. In February, as we trolled offshore, we spotted a swordfish swimming on the surface just about every day for a week. Jerry and Deborah Dunaway love to fish just as much as I did. So, after our 4:00 AM start every morning, we would try (not always successfully) to come in at 2:00 PM and take a nap, grab some dinner and head out to try to catch a swordfish. The first night out, we put out our two 130 pound outfits. We only had a couple of real squid, so we put those on the 130's. I wanted a smaller bait for the sixteen pound rod. We scrounged around and found some cuttlefish along the beach. A cuttlefish is a direct relative of the squid. They can be found in shallow waters and reefs and are often confused by divers and fisherman who see them in the shallow waters thinking they are squid. They were real small, so I put two on the hook and hesitantly let Deborah put the sixteen pound rod out. She let it out just a little ways, and set it in the holder. It couldn't have been five minutes and the sixteen pound started screaming off. We all looked at each other like, "What do we do now?" We cleared the two 130's and everybody took their positions. Fifteen minutes into the fight we got our first glimpse of the fish and it looked like a nice sized swordfish. It didn't really go anywhere and the next thing I knew, Mitch Scherfer, my deckhand, was grabbing the leader. The gaff man, Chito, planted the first gaff and I was off the bridge to help. We pulled the fish into the boat and to our surprise, it was a decent sized fish. The record book had no fish in the women's sixteen pound category. One hundred seventy-four pounds on sixteen pound line was world record for Deborah Dunaway.

We would see some of the best swordfishing for the next ten days that I have ever seen or heard of.. The following night we put out the 130's and caught two fish. We weighed them both and they came in at 220 and 180 pounds. I even cooked swordfish for the guests and staff at Tropic Star Lodge the next night!

The next night, February 19, 1986, we caught two more swordfish on 130 pound tackle. We tagged them as they were both only about 150 pounds each.

February 20th, we caught and released a 130 pound fish. During the day we were still catching sailfish, mahi-mahi and even a few striped marlin.

February 21st, we put out the twelve pound rods. It took only one bite and Jerry Dunaway was hooked up. Thirty minutes later a 166 pound swordfish was in the boat. These were the first two Swordfish that we caught on light tackle. I had heard all the stories of the long fights and pulled hooks with these great fish.

February 22nd , we let Deborah Maddox Dunaway try the twelve pound. We hooked up and after a one hour fight, we put a 112 pound swordfish in the boat. Another possible world record.

Jerry said he wanted to try one on eight pound line. The record was 106 pounds and was caught on six pound line. When the IGFA opened the eight pound line category, they merged the six pound line class into the eight pound line class. Of all of the swordfish that we caught so far, none were less than 100 pounds. Some were over 200 pounds. I was thinking that Jerry was really testing our psyche and we were getting real tired. Oh well, whatever the boss says.

Well, we put the two baits out on eight pound rods and it wasn't long before one was off and running. Jerry got situated in the harness and we all sat back for a long night quick break-off. You may as well be comfortable was our theory. One hour into the fish, we looked back about thirty yards and we could see the green light stick. The crew got ready and the next thing I knew, Mitch had the leader again and Chito sank the gaff. Could this be true? Another possible record?

We got to the dock and put the fish up on the scales. One hundred eight pounds. I felt bad for the guy who caught the prior record as he caught his fish on six pound line, twenty-five percent less breaking strength. He wrote Jerry a letter congratulating him and told us that he caught his fish in the daytime off Cabo San Lucas, Mexico. It took him five hours and he was very proud of this feat, and should be! Now he was heart broken and probably upset with the IGFA for this unfair change. Well, after a couple years, the IGFA reinstated the six pound records and he got his well deserved record back.

We went on that week to catch eight more fish and tagged most of them. One night the boss said that he was taking the night off, but that the good news was that he was going to let Marc Girard and John Paul Richard use the boat. We caught three swordfish that night along with a sailfish, a mahi-mahi, and a hammerhead shark. All but two swordfish were caught on eight pound line. The swordfish we caught on the eight pound line was too small and was tagged and released.

We did catch a 386 pound swordfish for Gary Price fishing out of Tropic Star Lodge a few years later. And that was our biggest in that area.

SOUTH AFRICA

When my Boss (Dick & Marg Love) called and told me we were going swordfishing in South Africa for two weeks, I knew then, that with all my travels, I still have a lot more to learn. Then he faxed me the results of the past two seasons of fish that were caught or tagged and released. The average weight was over 100 kilos, and the numbers were staggering! I was so excited that I ran down to the marine store and bought a chart just to get an idea of where they were fishing and what the weather was like. I really thought I was in for a rough ride going fishing off the Cape of Good Hope.

Then I started to think about all the things I was going to need because Dick said we were going to fish light tackle. First on my list was a top wireman/deckhand, and I got Scott "Squid" Levin. Then I started gathering the tackle, eighty-one pound, twelve pound, sixteen pound, and twenty pound. Then he told me we were fishing a tournament and I was an angler so I grabbed a 130 pound for me! Three suitcases later I was ready to go.

Soon my thoughts turned to the times we fished for swords so successfully off Miami in the late 1970's. The excitement of drifting at night and not knowing or seeing what size fish or even what kind of fish you might catch or battle for a while. There was rarely a night when we didn't get a bite. I was hoping it was the same over there.

Upon our arrival in Cape Town, we were picked up by our now good friend, Harry Laprini, and taken to our beautiful condo in Gordon's Bay. This is when I found out that we don't fish in the lee of Cape Town, we fish down off the Cape where you hear of all the rough seas and sunken boats. The weather was cool and breezy and we were informed we wouldn't be fishing that night, so we just worked on tackle, enjoyed the local beer, met the crew and looked at our Game Boat the *Broadbill*. She was twenty years old and looked like something Zane Gray and Lou Marron might have used for these same fish! The captain was Arnold Michels. His good friend, Wyn de Wet, was his number one crew, and John John John was his number two. I must have asked them fifty questions in the first twenty minutes, along with fifty more questions from my crew. Later Harry took us out to dinner where his wife, Helen, joined us. The food was great. Here we were in South Africa (after hearing and reading about the riots) enjoying a great dinner in this beautiful clean town and talking and dreaming about these swordfish! I was loving this!

The weather was still bad the following day, so we figured it was time to find the golf courses and arranged to play. On the course that morning we noticed the wind was calm and we knew we would be going that night.

We left the dock at 2:30 P.M. for the forty-eight mile run to the spot grounds. With our spirits running high we didn't expect to not get a bite, but it happened. We fished till 4:00 A.M. and headed home to get some sleep and try again later. Where were they?

The next night they found us (or we found them) and Dick hooked up on sixteen pound only to break the line forty-five minutes later. Another bite at 10:15 P.M. and another at 11:30 P.M. which broke the line. At midnight we had another hookup with Dick on sixteen pound which he fought hard only to break the line six hours later. Heartbreaker!

I remember fighting these fish on eighty and 130 pound line for hours, and then the fish only weighing 200 pounds. Were we out of our league? I was with Jerry and Deborah Dunaway when we caught four records in ten days on eight, twelve and sixteen pounds, so I knew it was possible. But here I saw Dick pull as hard as he could on sixteen pound test for six hours and the fish was pulling harder. I've read the Zane Grey books about his battles with these fish. They are the real gladiators of the sea.

The next night it blew so we got some rest and worked on our tackle and talked about the fish and drank some great South African wines.

On our sixth night there, and our third night fishing, two days before the tournament, we were out again. The wind was blowing ten to fifteen knots when we got out, but the waves were only two to three feet with a nice ground swell and we were ready.

By 8:30 P.M. we had a few squid bites and one UFO. The water seemed warmer. It was dark blue and hard to see down. The moon was up but not quite full and the wait was on. At 8:30 P.M. we had a screaming strike on the twelve pound line. Marg picked it up and the fight began. We also had a few guests out with us so the lines were cleaned easily and gaffs were ready. Barely five minutes had passed and I could see a lightstick on the surface a hundred or so yards out. Marg's twelve pound line still was angled down so she pulled, wound, and pulled some more 'til she got the belly of line out and tight to the fish. This nice old boat would only backup at about two to three knots which is sufficient, but slow from my view. As we came back the fish just stayed there. I don't know if the fish was gagging or what, but I knew this was our chance. We slowly came back and the twelve foot leader popped up into Scott's gloved hand. With a good double wrap and a quick move (a job well done) the fish was within the gaffs and Dick started them off. By the time I got down off the bridge to help, the crew had three gaffs in the fish and were screaming that the fish was over 200 pounds, a possible record. All I could do was congratulate Marg and tell myself that we did it. We pulled the fish in and celebrated and fished 'til midnight, when the winds were blowing twenty to twenty-five knots and we called it quits. The weigh-in was great. The crew had called their friends and fellow swordfishermen to see this. The fish weighed 120.8 kilos or 264.75 pounds. We broke the old record of 114 pounds by 150 pounds. The people couldn't believe it. They told me stories about fighting them on eighty pound line for two hours and the fish only weighed 100 kilos. They were amazed and so was I! After one bottle of champagne it was time to re-group and get some sleep.

We checked the weather at 2:00 P.M. and the crew said it was okay to try again. It was really nice out, but only one bite and it seemed the current had died. I was trying to find them again. The next night was the tournament kick off party so we got the rest we needed and met some of the nicest bunch of competitors I've ever met. They had a lot of questions for us, not only from my swordfishing reputation, but from what we've learned out locally. They did a bait rigging seminar and, for a tournament, these guys weren't keeping any secrets. They went out of their way to help each other before, during and after each day of the tournament. This was different for me. Now all there was to do was hope that the weather holds.

The first night out was nice, wind ten to fifteen, seas two to three foot with an eight foot swell with twelve boats fishing. (Thirteen in the tournament). We started fishing at 6:00 P.M. and at 6:42 P.M. we had out first strike. Dick was hooked up on sixteen pound line. After ten minutes the fish headed for the surface, as Dick was gathering line. I saw the fish jump off to the port side. We still had some belly, but we were close. Then again he jumped, and everyone saw him this time. But he went down before we got close. Fifteen minutes later we got the leader only to pull the hook before we could gaff her. We estimated the fish at 150-200 pounds, not big enough for a record on sixteen pound line. We put the baits back out and a few minutes later Marg's twenty pound rig went off. It was 7:46 P.M. and Marg was hooked up. The belly came out and the fish was swimming down sea. We got the leader and the gaffs found their mark., and at 8:05 P.M. the fish was in the boat! Record number two for Marg. We called it in and the congratulations came in.

By midnight we had no more bites and the wind picked up to twenty to twenty-five knots. I thought they would call it then. By 2:15 A.M. we had enough and started home. It was rough! Half the fleet had quit too and the few remaining were talking about it. Six hours later we got to the harbor having taken a good beating all the way home. (We had a small electrical fire and took on lots of water. I told Marg to put a couple of life jackets on the fish and rod in case we went down because I didn't want her to lose this record now).

At the scales we weighted our fish in at 128.4 kilos (282.5 pounds). There was one tagged and one other small one weighed in the tournament. We caught a record and were in the lead! Wow!

The next night was called off because of the winds. We were treated to a great curry dinner at the Club and a small birthday party of Dick and Dirty Harry!

On the sixth we were on our way out again. By 6:00 P.M. we had our baits out and at 6:15 had our first bite on twelve pound test. After ten minutes and a long run the line went slack. Another light tackle broken line.

We put the baits out right away and by 6:35 were hooked up again, this time on sixteen pound test with Dick as our angler. About fifteen minutes later we got the leader and the hook pulled. We got a real good look at the fish and with better lighting might have even had a gaff shot. We estimated the fish at 250 pounds. The current record is 243.

We licked our wounds and slowly put the baits out. The fleet was having good action too as four other boats were hooked up. Right at 7:00 P.M. off went the sixteen pound rig and Dick was hooked up again! As we were fighting this fish, the bite in the fleet went off Big Time. At least that's what it sounded like to me on the bridge being right next to the radio.

We got real close to this fish after an hour and in the shadow in the lights it looked like a real nice fish. Dick fought the fish as hard as he and the sixteen pound line would let him. By 4:00 A.M., nine hours later, I thought the fish was tired by her movements. Dick was concentrating so hard that he didn't know so many hours had passed. It was just him and that fish!

We had seen the light stick five or six times and had it so very close to Scott's heavily gloved hand. But with only fifteen feet of leader, we could only get it so close. It looked like inches but it still had a long way to come.

By 6:00 A.M. Dick looked like Mohammad Ali had hit him for eleven rounds and when the twelfth round started it wasn't getting any better. Dick was still giving it his best but he was tired. About 6:45, with the sun starting to rise, the fish made a 400 yard run, and after fifteen minutes, the fish was back within forty feet when the line gave out. Needless to say, it was a long, sad ride home. The fish won this one and Dick had done his best.

Back at the dock we told our story and listened to their's. There were thirty-six hookups and seven fish caught. Four weighed and three tagged. We decided to go home and get some much needed sleep.

On the third and final night of the tournament the seas were calm and we were ready. We had the baits in the water at 6:00 P.M., and it wasn't too long after that, that the fleet was calling in hookups.

At 7 P.M. we had our first bite. Marg hooked up on the sixteen pound rig. Could she go three for three? After ten minutes or so I looked way out and saw a lightstick. The belly in the line was coming up and came tight. So we started coming back. When we got close enough for me to see the fish in the lights, my knees started to shake. It looked like a nice one, 400 pounds or better! Scott reached out and grabbed the leader and the fish bolted up the side of the boat. By the time I could see this and react with the boat, the fish spun around and dove. When it all came tight and with Scott flat on the covering board, the hook pulled. Marg had done her job and the fish won this time. Just another part of the "Light Tackle Blues". All we could do now was to put those baits out again.

At 7:35 P.M. my 130 pound outfit went off. I finally get my turn! (I call it Revenge of the Nerds.) I got in the chair and put some drag on. We had questioned the chair earlier and now was the test.

About two minutes later I yelled, "Timber," as I fell over in the chair. We stood it up with the foot rest on the deck and John, the mate, stood on the base of the stanchion. With a curved butt 130 pound you can't stand up with just the rod. But with the chair angled like it was, I was fighting this fish standing up, and it was tough. After a thirty minute fight (I still don't know how we catch them on the light tackle) we switched the gaffs for the tag stick and back and forth a few times. When we finally got the leader and saw the size of the fish, I decided to tag it as it was only about 120 kilos. It wasn't the biggest of the tournament, so I decided to let her live even though we needed the extra points. It felt good!

After a short while we were hooked up again with Dick on the sixteen pound gear. We got close once and after twenty-five minutes, the line broke. Oh well, put the baits out. At 10:45 my 130 pound rig went off and it was my turn again. Into the broken stand up chair I went. The fish stayed close for a while and then, like the powerful fish that they are, it made a very long run, 300 yards plus, then the line went slack. I reeled it up only to find out the hook had pulled.

The action was slowing down for the fleet around midnight, but the earlier action was awesome and our hopes were still high. It was 2:30 A.M. when my 130 pound rig went off, and into action I went. After ten minutes the fish made a good run and I told the crew to ready the gaffs. "It feels big," I told them. I pumped the fish right to the boat after that run and when we got the leader and saw it was only about seventy pounds. The crew was laughing so hard at my big one that they could barely tag it. I took a good ribbing for that one the rest of the night. Oh well! At the weigh-in we found out that there were forty-five hookups and ten fish were tagged or caught. What a night!

The tournament was over and the awards were going to be on Sunday. This was Saturday morning and the weather was calm. At 2:30 P.M. we were on our way out again. Our last chance. We had the baits in the water at 6:30 and waited. It was 7:30 when we got our first bite and things got strange. The line broke right away and would again on the next two bites. Was it the line or the clip in the down rigger? All three were on twelve and sixteen pounds and were frayed and cut. (Maybe there were just too many fish down there and they were running into each other.) The light tackle blues were settling in big time.

At 9:30 we finally got to fight one for thirty minutes until the line broke. We had retied and re-spooled everything after the first one and it was really getting to us now! At 10:30 P.M. we hooked up with Dick on the sixteen pound gear. After twenty-five minutes and a great fight we caught one about sixty pounds. Success, but no record.

Marg hooked up at 11:15 on sixteen pound test and, after thirty-five minutes the line broke. The fish was close and she was pulling hard so we didn't feel bad. At midnight Marg hooked up again on sixteen pounds and after ten minutes we got close and the fish sounded. About twenty minutes later we got the leader but the hook pulled. The fish was only about 100 pounds and not a record so we gave her a WP release and a job well done.

At the awards on Sunday, Marg got Top Woman Angler. I got Second Place Angler with two tags and Top Release Angler. We congratulated the winners and held our heads high! Two World Records in six nights with twenty four bites was more than anyone could ever expect. The biggest fish in the town was 188 kilos by Peter Matthews and top boat was *Marauder* with three fish and lots of points.

We couldn't have asked for more. The hospitality, boats, rooms, and all the new friends made it really special. And a very special thanks to Dick and Marg for making all this possible. I can't wait til next year!

The totals for the tournament were:

13 boats

95 hookups

14 weighed

10 tagged and released

7 released

Captain
Bark Garnsey

©Kevin Nakamaru

CAPTAIN BARK GARNSEY

Known on the dock as "Bark," Capt. Thomas Barkley Garnsey was born in Alexander Bay, NY and grew up in Florida. Now however he lives in Silver City, New Mexico, 700 miles from the sea, not exactly the center of blue water activity. But for Capt. Garnsey it matters little because this world-wandering skipper spends so mush of his time in the most remote boondocks of the globe that one more relatively short flight on the long trip home is inconsequential.

Bark and angler Stuart Campbell have re-written the billfish record books on major expeditions to tropical backwaters. The pair have been so successful that many of their blue marlin records are now considered too hard to beat by even the likes of Skip Smith and Jerry Dunaway. Consider these records if you will – an 820 pound blue on sixteen pound line, and an 842 pounder on thirty pound line.

Garnsey's father, Capt. Dan Garnsey, guided summertime anglers to muskie and bass in the Thousand Islands of the St. Lawrence River. During the winter he fished commercially for king mackerel out of Florida's Hillsboro Inlet. The family migrated north and south with the seasons until the early 1950's when they settled in Pompano Beach, Florida.

Bark's father was his first and greatest teacher, and each summer Capt. Dan would take the family on a vacation trip through the Bahamas on his boat *Helen S*. Besides the closer Bimini and West End, destinations also included Walker's Cay (whose waters yielded Capt. Garnsey's first large blue marlin), the Abacos, the Exumas and Cat Island.

Bark's strongest memory of fishing was the capture of a world record swordfish which the five year old Bark witnessed while sitting beside the dry stack exhaust protruding through the roof of the old single screw drift boat.

Bill Knight, Billy Baum, Joe Mot, John Mumford and Allen Merritt, Danny Beare and just watching the "Greeks", Bill and George Staros, added to Garnsey's knowledge and skill as a young fisherman.

Tested Mettle

Bark's courage was really tested in Vietnam where he flew helicopters ("More fun to drive than a Merritt"). He was shot down five times while collecting a chest-full of medals including two Bronze Stars, two Distinguished Flying Crosses, a Silver Star, a Purple Heart, and a Vietnamese Cross for gallantry.

Though Bark's favorite fishing is for giant bluefin tuna in the Bahamas, his favorite fish story concerns a big black marlin fight.

He was alone with his now wife Carolyn on a seventy-foot Striker off Australia's Great Barrier Reef. They hooked a huge black marlin. "We got a 920 pound black marlin - on 100 pound . . . girl, that is," Bark laughs. "Not bad for just the two of us."

Besides being a superb fisherman, Capt. Garnsey has the organizational skills needed to get boats, tackle and every conceivable spare part to places like Java, Indonesia, Roatan, Honduras, San Pedro, Ivory Coast and the cape Verde Islands. Garnsey's atlas of fishing spots includes the east coast from Florida to Newfoundland, all of the Bahamas, Turks and Caicos, Puerto Rico, Virgin Islands, Windward Islands, Venezuela, Mexico, Panama, Brazil, Thailand, New Guinea, the Canary Islands and Madeira.

NICKY CAMPBELL'S MADEIRA ADVENTURE
by
BARK GARNSEY

So I am driving down the road minding my own business and this Pat Mansell guy, who I don't know from Adam, calls me on my magic phone and says he wants me to write a fishing story in this book. Two things come immediately to mind, one is I hate to write, a carry over from my less than stellar scholastic career, and the other is, how do I tell just one fish story? Fishing stories are like potato chips: you can't have just one, and they are better with a few beers. Since I have been fishing since about the time Moses was a mountain climber, in those many years I have come up with a fish story or two; so how can I pick the one I like the best? Hell, I can't speak for everybody, but I like all of them. So while I pondered this dilemma, I fell back on one of my strongest character traits, procrastination, and hoped that the tenacious Mr. Mansell would forget that he ever heard my name. Unfortunately for all concerned, he did not.

For over twenty years I have had the good fortune of running various boats for Mr. Stewart Campbell, a gentleman whose name will be familiar to anyone who has followed sport fishing in the last two decades. I have also had the privilege of working with several of the greatest mates and captains in the business, some of whom are in this book. Through the years, one of the greatest lessons that I have learned is that as individuals we can be fairly adept at something, but when we work together as a team we can be damned good at it. So I guess this story is as much about a bunch of guys and one "gal" working as a team as anything else.

In the late eighties and early nineties, Stewart, the mates, and I, who would come to be known in the trade as the "Over the Hill Gang," were fishing primarily in Venezuela with a few side trips to Brazil and other places. In the spring, and sometimes in the fall of every year, we would go to the Ivory Coast in West Africa for a month or more each trip. Trust me when I tell you that you have to want to catch a marlin pretty badly to spend a month or so in West Africa. In the early nineties the fishing was starting to slow down a little, and we started to look for greener pastures. We had made a trip to the Cape Verde islands in the summer of 1992 and had great fishing, so we decided to put together a boat to ship there. Before we could finish building a forty-four foot Garlington, the *Chunda*, we changed our minds. Ultimately we shipped her to the Canary Islands, about 850 miles northeast of the Cape Verde's. This was a fortuitous decision for us, because there we were befriended by some of the finest fishermen and gentlemen that we have ever known. It also put our base of operations only 300 miles from Madeira.

Most sport fishing enthusiasts have read or heard about the fantastic blue marlin fishing in Madeira in the mid 1990's. I can only say that if I had not had the incredible good fortune to be there in the summers of 1994, 1995, 1996, I would never have believed it myself. This was a run of blue marlin with an average size in excess of 600 pounds with an occasional "monster" fish thrown in for good measure. For the small handful of fishermen that were there, it was indeed a privilege to be party to that amazing time in fishing history.

The *Chunda* crew was made up of Mr. Stewart Campbell, his lovely wife Nickie, Charles Perry, Spencer Stratton, and me. Charles (aka CP), Spencer and I had worked together for quite some time. Although I may be a little bit prejudiced because we had been good friends for so long, I would be hard pressed to find two better men to have in the cockpit at any time. In the summer of 1994, Stewart talked about putting away the light tackle and trying to catch a real big one on eighty pound test. After several years of trying to catch blue marlin on very light line, it did not take us long to say, "HELL YES!" We did manage to take an 1,143 pound fish that came up tail wrapped. No small feat on eighty pound line, and a lot harder for

Stewart than for the rest of crew. Early in the summer of 1995, Stewart got the itch to try and better his standing world record on thirty pound. Personally speaking, I was quite happy with the heavy stuff, but I had not lost sight of the fact that he was paying the bills. In late August of that year, with Capt. Marty Snow filling in for Spencer, and Guy Harvey along to make sure we did it properly, Stewart caught an 872 pound blue marlin on thirty pound to beat his own record for the second time. At that point I would have been happy to donate the old thirty pound rig to the first pier fisherman I came across. But alas, the summer of 1996 found us with the thirty still onboard, and to make it even worse, Stewart was thinking that we could catch a "grander" on the thirty pound. Mr. Perry could not agree more. I should add that anyone that knows CP well will tell you that he is as crazy as a shit house rat when it comes to pulling on a leader wire. Spencer and I, who are very slightly older than CP, and much wiser, just shook our heads knowingly and tried to talk some sense into our shipmates, and asked for a vote. Nickie refused to vote because she thinks we are all nuts anyway. Ties always go to the owner, so off we charged with our skimpy little thirty pound rig held at port arms. Sure enough, just a few days later, up came a marlin that all on board agreed was well over a grand and we got him on. Things were looking real good, and we were thinking that we might just catch this great beast, when Stewart decided to change sports.

As most people in the fishing business know, and thousands of other folks who have seen Charles Perry's video, *Cockpit Chaos*, discovered, this was the point where Stewart went from doing a great job as an angler to doing a fair job as a swimmer. Actually he must not have done too bad a job of swimming, because he managed to avoid being ground up by a very large set of propellers. Stewart climbed back in the boat somewhat the worse for wear, with a dislocated finger, split lip, two black eyes, various bumps and bruises and in need of a few stitches. People who don't know Stewart might think we would take a few days off to lick our wounds. Those who do know Stewart, know that we went fishing the very next day. Although Stewart was fishing with a soft cast on his left hand, he caught one about 700 pounds.

The next day we started talking about Nickie getting in the chair. We had had our eye on the women's world record on thirty pound test line. This record was set by Gloria Gray on May 20, 1989 and the fish weighed 560 pounds. To be totally honest about it, the fact that the captain on the catch was a fellow named Skip Smith encouraged us even further. Some of you readers may have heard his named mentioned a time or two before. Skip and his crew were "the force" to be reckoned with at the time, so anytime you could snatch one from those guys, it was just a little bit sweeter. We had snatched a couple in earlier days and they were just as likely to snatch them right back. It was a friendly competition with guys that we had a great amount of respect for.

Before I go any further with this fish story, I need to explain something, if I might. We use a method of fishing known as bait and switch. Simply stated, we pull four lures with no hooks. When a fish comes up, we pull the lure toward the boat and as soon as possible, estimate its weight. You may have three or four rods with different line test, baited and ready to flip over the stern. Fishing in this manner, a fish of 300 pounds that on heavy tackle would be just another fish, could be a potential record on a lighter line. The downside to this for the angler and crew is that you don't get a lot of practice. You don't have for example, any spring training, or regular season games. Bang! You go right straight to game seven of the World Series.

So, after solemn promises that we would not let her get pulled overboard, Nickie agreed to give it a try. Stewart immediately went to work coaching her on dropping back, getting in the chair, drag settings, when to back way off the drag when the fish is jumping or rapidly taking line, and about 100 other things. Nickie had fished almost every day with us through the years, but mostly she took pictures and kept the galley sorted out so, to her, this was indeed a daunting task.

The very next day found us fishing again with the added incentive of finding a marlin in the 550-700 pound class for Nickie. The first day proved a total wash, but anyone who has spent much time marlin fishing takes that in stride. The plus side was it gave Stewart more time to help Nickie settle into her new role as angler. The next day was very different; boy was it ever. Madeira is usually calm, but this day was even flatter than most. Mike Latham, a good friend, who was working with Capt. Bobby Brown, took a busman's holiday and came along with us in hopes of shooting some video. Before noon we raised a fish that was about the right size, and Nickie hooked it straight away. Just as quickly the line broke. When someone is trying to do something that has never been done before, e.g. a women catching a 600 pound marlin on thirty pound line, you have to allow them some mistakes. Having said that, the only trouble was, she had not done anything wrong, and as far as we could tell there was no reason for the line to break. The worse thing that can happen on a sport fishing boat is a damn "mystery." Stewart tied a new double line and we started over. Minutes later Mike, who was in the tower with me, saw a nice fish cutting bait on the surface about ¼ mile away. As we trolled the lures through the fresh slick on the surface, I asked Mike which way should I go, left or right. Mike commented that I was putting a lot of pressure on him. I told him not to worry because if he was right I would take the credit, and if he was wrong, I would blame it on him (so much for being a nice guy). Mike said, "Turn right!" And sure enough he was right. Man, this was a nice fish. I got so excited I did not have time to steal the credit from Mike. This fish was near a grand, so I told Stewart to throw the thirty pound. This fish was nearly the size of the fish that had taken Stewart for a swim a few days earlier. She followed the lure and made a nice handoff to Stewart's mackerel and then stopped right there and swam along behind the bait. We had seen this several times with very big fish. I guess they don't get that big being stupid. This fish faded away, and while we were arguing about how big she was, up popped another one. I told Nickie to try this one on the thirty pounds and everything went like clockwork until she put it in gear. Once again the line popped. We all huddled in the cockpit and decided to dump the line off and spool on new line, even though we knew the line was good. And so we solved the "mystery." The day before, we had Nickie practicing throwing the bait and free spooling several times. Occasionally we would drop the bait back fairly far and wind the line back on. This was done at about an eight knot lure trolling speed because, although we were practicing, we were also still fishing. *When you are winding the bait in, it will often skip or jump toward the boat and cause loops of slack line to get wound in the spool. It will happen with ballyhoo at a slow trolling speed on light line. It is even worse with larger bait at a higher speed.* This was something that Nickie didn't need to know, but the rest of us did. Unlike some marlin, we were able to get bigger and still be stupid.

New top shot on the reel, new leader and new bait and we were ready to give it another try. This was a type of fishing where it was better for your mental health to have a short memory. Twenty minutes later a fish popped up that I was fairly sure was not big enough for a record, but obviously we needed the practice. Spencer teased the fish up and made a perfect handoff. Nickie hooked it like she had been doing it every day and the line did not break. Twenty minutes later CP wired up a fish about 450-500 pounds, and Spencer cut the leader right at the corner of her jaw and she swam away. Life was good again onboard the *Chunda*. Nice job on thirty pound line and everybody was feeling better about our chances. Thirty minutes later up came another fish, and this time I thought it would make the weight. Once again Spencer made a perfect handoff, and Nickie hooked up again. This time the level of excitement was higher because this could be the one we needed for a record. Stewart was turning the chair and coaching his ass off. Remember, these were IGFA rules, and no one but Nickie could touch anything on the rod, reel or line. These were the rules and they were pretty damn simple. *I hope that everyone that fishes for records or in tournaments lives by them. Excuse me for a moment while I step down from this soapbox.*

One thing that we had learned through the years was that if a fish was jumping or taking line fast, you had better back off the drag quickly. With light line it was even more critical, and with the speed that a blue marlin generates before and during a jump, you almost needed to be in free spool. For the first few minutes of the fight this fish jumped all over the ocean but did not get too far away from the boat. Now she took off on a blistering jumping run across the surface. I yelled down that I was coming around and spun the boat toward the fish as she smoked line off the reel. Everyone knows that boats go faster frontward than backwards, so if you needed to get there in a hurry, you would point the bow at the fish and haul ass. When I said I was coming around, Stewart knew immediately that he needed to start back with the drag, and if the fish was jumping he would come back almost to free spool. The problem here, of course, was that Stewart was not in the fighting chair, Nickie was. Stewart immediately told Nickie what she needed to do, but unfortunately she came back a little too far. What can I say, the kid was a rookie, she was doing some pretty work but things were happening real fast. So now we had a very large backlash, but because the boat was moving toward the fish faster than the fish was moving away, the line had not broken, YET. I shouted down and asked if we could overcome it. By this I meant if I could keep the line slack, could Nickie pick the tangle out of the line. The answer back was the worst three part harmony I have ever heard. "NO WAY!" Due to an ingenious little device that Shimano had installed on our reels, I was also informed that we had fifty-eight yards of line to work with before we came to the backlash from hell. Now we had nothing to lose, so I figured, what the hell; let's go for it. Man was that fun. We spun and ran so many times I lost count, and more than once came within inches of the backlash and disaster. I have no idea how long it took, it seemed like hours, but CP finally got the leader with no plans of letting go. At the last minute I called down that I didn't think she was big enough, and we should let her go. Let me say right here that my mates could have had veto power over that decision; they were a lot closer to the fish than I was. Plus, according to my buddy, Skip Smith, I would be better off trying to guess their age than their weight. However, since the mates didn't disagree, we released her, and quickly went back fishing. In the next fifteen or twenty minutes both CP and Spencer climbed up in the tower and told me they thought she was probably big enough for the record. I was sure Mike Latham agreed wholeheartedly. Command is indeed a lonely position, and to make it even worse, they were probably right. On second thought, maybe Skip was also.

Luckily for me, before my fine crew could carry through with any mutinous plans they might have been plotting, we raised another fish. This one was big enough with plenty of pounds to spare. Spencer teased her right up, and Nickie hooked it just as nice as you please. This was getting to be old hat for her. This fish put on a show right from the bite, and the chase was on. Nickie had no backlashes to worry her this time, and Stewart was right over her shoulder to keep her calm and focused. I could have used a little help on that front myself. What with mysterious broken lines and horrible backlashes, impending mutiny, and Mike Latham trying to beat me half to death in the tower, I was having a long day. This fish opened up a whole new bag of tricks. A couple of the boats in the fleet trolled over just to watch the show. And quite a show it was. She had all the moves that you could imagine, but she made one big mistake, she stayed on top. *With light line if fish will stay near the surface, you always have a chance. If they go down deep, it is another story altogether. They can be caught, but it takes a whole different program.* After forty-five minutes of tearing up a lot of water, and maybe a transmission or two, CP got the leader. The fish was going straight away, and I was trying to stay with her but still not cause too much commotion with the boat. CP reached out and took a really pretty backhand wrap, and then a double, and as calmly and smoothly as you could ever imagine, pulled her slowly toward Spencer's waiting flying gaff. Stewart came right over his shoulder with a second gaff because Mike was not dropping that camera for anything. As we slid her through the door, everyone agreed that she was the one we wanted. Since it was getting very close to "beer-thirty", we headed for the dock.

When we reached the marina, we slid the fish out the tuna door and towed her along side the concrete wall with a small skiff, where a waiting truck crane dropped a hook over to Spencer and me. Spencer and I had agreed beforehand that we would pretend that the fish was not big enough for a record just to tease Nickie. As I was holding the electronic scales in the boat, no one else could see the numbers until I turned them upward toward the crowd on the dock. We all knew that Nickie did not want to take any fish unless it was a record. She was pretty confident, but you never know for sure until you read the scales. As the fish came up, Spencer and I saw for sure that it was a record, well before the head and bill got out of the skiff. Being the real jerks that we are, we hung our heads in dejection as the fish cleared the boat. We slowly looked at Nickie and shook our heads, no. We kept up our deception for about two seconds and then let out a couple of good old rebel yells and turned the scales up for Nickie and everyone else to see: 708 pounds. That beat the old record by 148 pounds. Not a bad day's work for a little lady. As I looked up at Nickie, I could see a tear roll down her cheek as she accepted everyone's congratulations. Had anyone looked down into that small skiff they might have seen a tear or two there also.

The next day while fishing, Stewart came up into the tower for a chat. As we discussed our efforts of the previous day's fishing, I told him something then that I still believe is true today. We had caught some nice fish through the years in many different places and on many different boats. I truly believe that Nickie's fish was the best job of teamwork that we had ever done. At the end of the day, and even at the end of a career, it is more about the people that you were with, than the fish you have caught.

Captain
Billy Harrison

©Kevin Nakamaru

CAPTAIN BILLY HARRISON

Growing up in a Coconut Grove, Florida, young Billy Harrison had the best of all worlds. Right there in Dinner Key Marina there were bay shrimpers, commercial mullet and mackerel boats, lobster boats, head boats and charter boats all docked up together. Everyday during the winter Billy could ride his bicycle down to the dock and watch shrimp, grouper, turtles, sharks, lobsters, mackerels and so much more unloaded from the boats. Fishing there at a young age was a great experience and soon he moved on to the Chamber of Commerce Dock on South Miami Beach. There he learned from great captains like Red Stuart and his brother Bob on the *San Donna* and *Sea Quest*. Later from the Castaways Charter Boat Dock on North Miami Beach, Billy fished with Connie Myra on the *Connie M II*. Connie was the first lady to run a charter boat out of South Florida. Billy spent time at the Crandon Park Charter Boat Dock, fishing with Jimmy O'Neille on the *Queen B.*

But the most famous charter boat dock in the world at the time was Miami's Pier Five. There Billy fished and learned from the legendary Buddy Carey. Buddy owned and ran his charter boat, *Sea Boots* out of Miami starting in 1937. He also bluefin tuna fished out of Cat Cay with the famous "Greeks," Bill and George Staros.

As a teenager in South Florida, Billy fished the Bahamas every spring and summer. Later he added Puerto Rico, St. Thomas and Mexico to his list followed soon thereafter by Venezuela, Central and South America. He next expanded his territory to include frequent trips to Hawaii and the South Pacific, along with Cape Cod, Prince Edward Island and Bermuda.

Starting in the early 1980's, Billy spent the entire black marlin season in the mother ship operations off Australia's Great Barrier Reef. Here he fished with Peter Bristow onboard *Avalon*. In 1991 he split the black marlin season, fishing the first half with Peter Bristow and then finished the season with Peter Wright on the *Duyfken*. Throughout his career Billy made twelve trips to Africa. Some of these African adventures included fresh water fishing the Zambesi River for Tigerfish where herds of as many as 100 elephants wade and swam around the boat.

Billy grew up in the era where killing hundreds of blue, black, striped and white marlin, along with sailfish, swordfish and bluefin tuna was an expected part of the job. As a commercial fisherman, he was involved in the early parts of longlining swordfish off the Florida coast. For twenty-five years he owned a deep water snapper and grouper boat which fished for tilefish and grouper. As the times and attitudes changed toward the releasing of marlin and tuna, so did Billy, and in 1986 he was awarded the NOAA and National Coalition for Marine Conservation's highest award for tagging the most marlin of any captain during that year.

As a writer and photographer, many of Billy's articles and pictures have been used in Marlin Magazine, Sportfishing Magazine, Saltwater Sportsman Magazine and many European magazines along with Ski-Boat Magazine out of South Africa. Famous Australian author, Peter Goadby, features over a dozen of Billy's photos in his great book, Saltwater Gamefish. Through the years, Billy has had his photos used in fifteen different calendars published yearly around the world. Living in Miami, Billy Harrison continues to tuna fish out of Cat Cay every year and finds time to fish a few tournaments in the Bahamas and St. Thomas.

BLUE FINS OFF BIMINI
by
BILLY HARRISON

While walking down the old wooden docks of the Bimini Big Game Club in the predawn hours, I could tell that today's conditions were perfect for bluefin tuna fishing. It was Friday, May 21, 1976 and I was the captain of the thirty-seven foot, diesel powered Merritt named *Miltown III*. My Bahamian mate was Copperhead Rolle and Scottie Taylor, my other mate, was from Miami, Florida. The angler on board for the two week charter was one of the most colorful fishermen I have ever encountered. His name was Yohannes Hekimian.

Yohannes had a most colorful past. He was born in Addis Ababa, Ethiopia, and during his illustrious career as a Special Forces officer, was noticed for his exceptional strength, loyalty and dedication. On account of that, he rose through the ranks to become a personal bodyguard to the great historic figure, King Haile Selassie. During those years Yohannes would accompany the King on safaris through Africa, hunting wild lions and elephants. He was the last line of defense between any manner of wild man or beast and the Ethiopian regent.

Johannes's deformed fingers were his tools. Meaty palms and twisted fingers from so many broken bones, his and others, were met by bulky forearms and huge biceps. His shoulders were wide and his oversized head was shaved bald, showing muscles on the back side, and a large friendly smile on the front.

Every year a dedicated group of men and a few women would assemble at Cat Cay and Bimini to fish the bluefin tuna migration that lasted roughly one month. Of this group, Yohannes, with his old style European charm and great personality, was the best liked.

During the previous two weeks, the bluefin tuna fishing had been very good and, as I would later learn, the fishing would stay good for another thirty days. We were on a good roll of our own. For the last three days we had released one or more tuna each day averaging 500 to 700 pounds. Conditions were perfect. The current was flowing to the north with plenty of clean water, the skies were clear to partly cloudy and, most important, the wind was blowing from the southeast. So far during this May we had south or southeast wind every day. The forecast was calling for the wind to drop off later today, but there was a low pressure area on the way. This meant that the wind would start right back up, blowing out of the southwest in a day or two. My crew and I were impatient to go fishing today because we knew we had to be in early for some of our guests to make the last Chalks seaplane flight out of Bimini in the afternoon.

Copperhead Rolle was my spotter and Scottie Taylor worked the cockpit. I had great respect for Copperhead since he and I went back to the mid-sixties working together. Copper was only five feet six (so he said) and was a native Bahamian. His black hair was burned copper color by the brutal Bahamas sun. He had been a professional mate all his forty-six years and had worked with me in the Bahamas and St Thomas. I liked having him fish with me because I knew that I could always count on him and his good judgment. He was a true professional and absolutely one of the best in the cockpit. Being born in Bimini, he and his family had an interesting island history. On August 10, 1967 we helped his brother, Manny Rolle, unload a Bahamas ladies record 723 pound blue marlin on his charter boat *Gold Bill*. Manny would later open a grocery store across the street and a little to the south of the Big Game Club. It burned down twice in its twenty-five year history. His other brother was also famous for running the *Bimini Babe* for the Landwer family. They had a beautiful home just north of Pogie Bay on the harbor side of Bimini. His name was Shoestring Rolle. Shoestring's gigantic hands could pick up a bowling ball without putting his fingers in the holes. I made sure to stay good friends with Shoestring!

Copper and I had blue marlin fishing down perfect. Once the fish would get to the side of the boat, Copperhead would wire it and I would run down from the bridge and gaff it. Together we would then drag the fish through the door and across the deck. Blue marlin fishing was fun, but the real challenge to Copperhead was tuna fishing. He liked the boat-to-boat competition and had good eyes for spotting the northbound schools of tuna. What I most liked about Copper was his willingness to ride the tower all day long.

The other mate who worked the cockpit was Scottie Taylor. As a teenager, Scottie worked for me when I fished out of Pier Five in Miami, Florida. He had that youthful love of fishing and the desire to become better at it. He had a quick introduction to big game fishing when he joined me on a trip to St. Thomas during the summer of 1974. He went from catching amberjack, grouper and sailfish to suddenly wiring 300 and 400 pound blue marlin on a daily basis. Back in those days many of our clients wanted to have their beautiful marlin mounted so that it would be a showpiece in their home or on a wall in their office. This meant that Scottie, being the only mate, had to become a good wireman in a hurry. I give him credit for going to the really big name mates in St. Thomas and asking questions about wiring and gaffing blue marlin. Having a body weight of 140 pounds, Scottie had a serious disadvantage when a wild 500 pound blue was jumping at the side of the boat on the wire. As the days went by, he wired blue marlin after blue marlin and became better and better. He ended that summer of 1974 with more than fifty blue marlin to his credit. Compared to many of today's wiremen, this is a lifetime achievement.

Yohannes's friends were flying back to Texas that afternoon and he had promised them plenty of fresh tuna. I entered the restaurant at the Big Game Club and tried to explain to Rev. Pinder, the maitre d', that we needed to have our breakfast and box lunches as soon as possible. We then had one of the good but notoriously slow breakfasts served to us at the club restaurant. Finishing our meal, we waited and waited and waited and waited for our box lunches. This slowed our departure even more. Once we finally received our box lunches, we boarded the *Miltown III* and started out through the clear water of Bimini Harbor. The *Miltown III* had a hailing port of Houston, Texas and was the first thirty-seven foot Merritt to have small diesels installed. This meant that it was the absolute slowest boat in the fleet, roaring seventeen knots wide open.

I chose to take the short cut behind Turtle Rocks and Gun Cay in order to get us to Tuna Alley as quickly as possible. Approaching Gun Cay Channel, I went to the tower while it was still calm, followed by Copperhead. Since our relationship spanned most of my life, I enjoyed Copper's company in the tower for the eight or ten hours we spent looking for tuna each day. I usually ask my mates to wear a dark shirt when they ride the tower and to stay as low as possible so that I can see over them when we are baiting schools of tuna. Copper was perfect in the tower; he was short so I could easily see over him, and he was a native Bahamian, so the dark shirt was not necessary.

Ahead of me I could see five boats that were baiting schools of tuna and already there was one boat that had hooked-up and was offshore in the deep water doing battle with a tuna. Today was just like the previous seven days and the schools were marching up the edge, one after another, all on their way north. As we ran south into the wind and current, we watched the five boats go by in the opposite direction, all leading their schools of tuna on their way north. After passing the last northbound boat, I then slowed down, leaving a gap of several miles of open ocean before the next group of tuna boats to the south. Like magic, a school of northbound tunas showed up right on schedule and we now had our turn to try our tricks.

Copperhead and I divide our viewing area in half. He got the shallow water side to the east and I took the deep water side to the west. The shallows are anything from a depth of roughly sixty feet to one hundred feet on the Bahamas Bank. When the tunas are in the shallow water they can be seen for a great distance because their dark bodies stand out against the white sand. Even on the dark rocky patches of the shallows, the giant tuna definitely stand out from their surroundings. Our first school was in the deep water to the west and looked to be about the same distance off the edge as the other five schools that we had passed, except they had no escort boat to slow their rapid progress to the north.

Since the tuna boat is running south and the schools of tuna are swimming to the north, great care must be taken not to collide with the school and spook the front few fish thus sending the entire group down and out of sight. Once the school of tuna is spotted, the boat must come around and get into a position where one bait will be dragged at a sharp angle ahead of the northbound school. On our first school of the day, I came around on the east side of the tuna school and then ran north before slowing down to baiting speed. This is a standard type of operation for morning tuna fishing since the sun is still on the east side of Tuna Alley and the sun's rays help us to better see the fish to the west. Now we were in perfect position and Copper gave the signal to let the bait go. The signals are easy; one finger for a mullet, two for a mackerel, and a flat hand means try a flopper. The flopper is a big silver mullet weighing at least 1½ pounds that has had everything cut out of the inside and is about one half inch thick from the nose all the way down to the split tail.

It flops on top of the water and is usually fished at the short mark after the school of fish have been baited for a while and can be better controlled. Today the wind was blowing just over fifteen knots so we used six ounce chin leads to make the baits swim vertically.

The *Miltown III* was very quiet and threw a relatively small wake. This allowed us to bait the schools quite close under the right conditions. I fished the short mark at 150 feet and the long mark at 220 feet and always started with the long mark at the tip of the rod. As the school is worked and the fish can be better controlled, we then bait the tunas at the short mark. The hookup rate is higher at the short mark and the strikes are definitely more spectacular!

Baiting the first school proved futile. We tried mullet, mackerel, floppers and even an old squid that had been in the bait box so long that we felt it was part of the crew. I always spend too much time with the first school of the day, hoping to start things off with the 'big bite'. Reluctantly I gave up baiting this school since several of the other boats that we had passed earlier were now charging south along the edge jeopardizing my desirable position. Continually running south makes one think that the boat would end up 100 miles from home at the end of the day, but the geographic position of the boat only changes north and south over a twenty mile area. The tuna boats are continually swapping positions due to the fact that one boat runs several miles south at fifteen or twenty knots then, finding a school of tuna, turns and baits them to the north for several miles. Both the tunas and the Gulf Stream current, which the tunas ride, are moving to the north. Bluefin tunas usually swim at eight to ten knots and the Gulf Stream current usually flows at two, three and, sometimes four knots. While baiting the northerly swimming schools of blue fins, the combination of the two north moving objects accelerates their speed, so after fifteen minutes of baiting, a great distance is covered. If a tuna boat is baiting an exceptionally large school of fish, the captain might stay with this school for many miles. Getting the bait to every fish is difficult and takes a great deal of time. Once the captain gives up the school, he will again turn south and run until the next school is spotted.

We were baiting our third school without ever having a "looker". This is a bluefin that breaks out of formation and follows the bait the length of the school before returning to the northbound assembly of tunas. If the spotter shouts down to the cockpit crew that a looker is behind the bait, the excitement in the pit is increased with the anticipation of a tuna strike. The reality of tuna fishing is that the people in the cockpit almost always see the spectacular explosion of spray caused by the violent strike, since they are at eye level with the bait and are watching as the line goes straight back behind the boat. The two men in the tower rarely see the strike since they are keeping track of all fish in the school.

Once the baiting is started, the spotter runs the cockpit crew thus allowing the captain to devote full attention to working the boat and the school of tuna. While baiting this school, Copperhead informed me that another barracuda had chopped the bait in half. These cutoffs are one of the real frustrating parts of tuna fishing. As we lined up the fourth time to make a pass on the school, Copper gave the signal and the leaded mullet went over the side. When we were only two fish into the school, Yohannes's yell shook the boat. This yell sent Copper scurrying down the left tower leg into the cockpit while I brought the boat around to the deep water side of the hooked bluefin. This tuna behaved exactly as I would expect and streaked across the surface while the *Miltown III* came chugging behind. I saw the fish break water off the bow of the boat, and even though we were going foreword wide open, the line on our reel was rapidly being dumped. Finally the tuna dived and it was up to Yohannes to go to work. Since the tuna had now gone down, I left the tower in favor of the bridge controls. Ten minutes later

Yohannes looked up at me smiling and I knew that the tuna had finally stopped its dive to the deep water. Yohannes was about to switch and become the aggressor.

The 12/0 Fin-Nor spool on the reel never stayed still with Yohannes. It was either turning away as the tuna took line, or it was coming in as he would violently attack the fish and gain line inch-by-inch at any cost. He was known throughout the tuna fleet as a man who never sat in the chair and waited patiently. After gaining half of the four hundred yards of Dacron line back on the reel, the tuna abruptly rushed straight down taking back another hundred yards. Yohannes would stay airborne in the harness with sixty pounds of drag on the tuna until it stopped and, at this exact moment, he would go back to his wild attack with the drag on a full ninety pounds.

Having released every tuna we caught this week, we now planned to put this one in the boat. Yohannes's friends wanted fresh tuna to take home this afternoon. I could see Copperhead wearing his wiring gloves and Scottie laying out the straight gaff and safety rope that went to the fixed gaff head. Rarely did a tuna take the straight gaff out of the mate's hands, but I insisted on using the added safety rope. The mates would decide who would wire the first tuna of the day and from then on they would alternate if we caught more fish. Since the tuna was going to be put in the boat, one of Yohannes's friends was steering the fighting chair. The brutal Bahamian sun that beat down on Yohannes's muscled back caused the sweat to pour off his entire body as he pulled unmercifully on the tiring tuna. He had his own one gallon water jug that hung from the chair and was never put on ice. Sometimes in the harness, as he balanced high in the air, he would take a big gulp of warm water and then slosh a small amount over his bald head.

Finally the tuna started to pinwheel and Yohannes went into the kill mode. I knew there would be no more joking or laughing until the tuna was up to the surface. Copperhead, wearing the wiring gloves, walked to the starboard corner of the transom and looked down into the blue water. He was a good wireman. Being short, he could keep his thighs under the covering boards and then pull with a straight back. He now saw the glimmer of a hooked tuna deep down in the clear water. It was swimming in large pinwheel turns that allowed Yohannes to gain line on the upside of the circle. As the bluefin turned and started on the down side of the pinwheel, Yohannes would hold the 12/0 Fin-Nor spool and rise high in the air thus making me fear that he could possibly bend another footrest.

Scottie now had the gaff held vertically with the head pointing outboard. As Copper looked into the clear water, he turned toward me and said something inaudible, so I knew that the snap was only a few feet away. Once Copperhead grabbed the wire he would have complete control of the cockpit. Everyone including the gaff man would move out of his way. He would also determine when the tuna was ready to be gaffed. Once the wiring process started, these two professionals rarely spoke, even at critical times. As Copper pulled the twenty feet of number fifteen wire, Scott moved to the starboard corner of the cockpit and now held the gaff horizontal with the point facing down, directly over the up coming tuna's head. I maneuvered the boat so Copper would not have to move from his locked-in position four feet ahead of Scottie's starboard corner. I could see the tuna getting closer and closer. Copper finally took a double wrap and pulled the tuna's head to the surface as Scottie gaffed it under the pectoral fin. I waited until Copper looked up and gave a nod, then I made one of my rare trips to the cockpit deck. My job was to put the meat hook through the tuna's lower jaw which was easy since it was now on its back. Once I took the strain off Copper, he released the wire and opened the tuna door which, on a thirty-seven foot Merritt, is huge. We walked the fish aft and around the starboard corner and, with one easy pull, the bluefin slid through the door and across the teak cockpit floor.

Pulling a tuna into a thirty-seven foot Merritt is easy since the water level is just below the bottom of the door. As the three men went to the starboard side of the cockpit and pulled on the meat hook that was in the tuna's mouth, the waves helped wash the tuna through the door. Once our tuna was in the boat, I then shut the door and turned to Yohannes making a guess of 700 pounds before congratulating him with a handshake. Half way up the tower leg I looked down and saw Yohannes standing on the fighting chair seat with his arms straight up in the sky and his fists clinched. I knew some sort of victory yell would follow.

On the way back to the edge the two mates tied the tuna across the cockpit behind the fighting chair. There was still time to catch another tuna! In the thirty minutes that we had been involved with the tuna, the wind had dropped five knots but the sea kept its perfect roll. The entire tuna fleet had changed position. Some had run to the south, some had hooked-up and others, baiting big schools of tunas, were halfway to Bimini. The schools continued to show and, while baiting our third school of tuna, we got the bite! Copper had seen a big school up shallow and, while we baited the fish, I pushed them farther and farther into the shallows. After the bite, I came around and broke the school up. A group of around ten tunas ran north over the sandy bottom making it easy to follow our fish since he was in the middle of this group.

As I followed, staying on the deepwater side of this group, the unthinkable happened. We were cut off by a lobster trap. Somewhere during the quarter mile that we had run with the tunas, an underwater rope and submerged float had separated us from our second giant tuna of the day. This was a real letdown since catching a tuna up shallow is so much fun for everyone on board! Chasing a hooked tuna in the clear shallow sandy bottom makes everyone on board the boat appreciate how fast these great fish are as they race over the white sand.

Yohannes's favorite rod and reel, which was a modified "stump puller" filled with 200 pound test Dacron line, was now out of commission since the cut off line caused the marks to be no longer usable. We now broke out our standard tuna rod and reel. This is an unlimited rod with a 12/0 Fin-Nor reel filled with 130 pound test Dacron. We only had another hour to fish before turning north and heading home to Bimini. Looking down from the tower at Yohannes as he adjusted the new rig, I knew that a trip to the cockpit was necessary. I gave Copper the wheel and descended the right side tower leg to the bridge and then onto the cockpit deck. Knowing that I could not tell Yohannes to be patient with this new lighter tackle, I choose to simply remind him that a little less drag might be appropriate. After a short talk and several reminders that this was far lighter than his familiar tackle, he reluctantly agreed to be patient and then reminded me that I should be in the tower driving the boat and not down in the cockpit where I did not belong.

The wind had dropped to less than ten knots and the sea was now down to a small heave. The next tuna school that we spotted was not moving nearly as fast as the previous schools. Not wanting to go into Bimini with just one flag for the day, we made two more unsuccessful passes on the school with mullet. The last flooper that we tried drew a looker, but it quickly gave up the chase and returned to the northbound formation, and the entire school then disappeared somewhere into the deep blue water. We then returned to the edge, where I slowed the boat to an idle, went to neutral, and waited for the next formation of bluefins. After a short lull, I saw the next school of tunas on their way north. It appeared to be a small school, maybe a dozen fish. After coming around on them, I found their northward speed surprisingly fast, since the wind had died out and the sea had dropped to a gentle role. The tunas kept coming closer, and were already in our wake when Copperhead gave the signal. Once the bait was out and the mark was at the tip of the rod, I heard some muttering coming from the other side of the tower. I looked back at the bait and realized that the flopper was still being used from the previous school of tuna that we had just finished baiting. A flopper was Copper's least favorite bait and toward the end of the day he would let me know by continually grumbling whenever we used a flopper to bait a school of bluefins. Since we had caught many tunas together, I knew that telling Copperhead of our success rate while using floppers as baits would automatically bring a response of how many more strikes we had on mackerel, mullet and any other kinds of bait. At this point in the day it did not bother me in the least to try a flopper first. As I turned the boat to hack through the school, Yohannes's yell caught both of us standing in the tuna tower by surprise. Quickly looking back toward the bait, I saw a huge shower of white foaming water as tall as the top of our tuna tower. I learned later that two tuna had both lunged for the surface bait and their colliding bodies had caused the huge eruption of spray. The angler and cockpit crew are always in the best position to enjoy these spectacular surface strikes.

Being headed offshore, the boat was at a good angle and a perfect position to come around on the fish, but the farther I turned the boat, the more southerly the tuna ran. At one point, the bluefin went a full one hundred yards, throwing ten feet of white foaming water from its tail while running straight south. Since the sea had only a gentle roll and we were going to release this one, I stayed in the tower. The tuna finally stopped running across the surface and headed for the depths. Taking four or five hundred yards of line, it finally stopped and held its position. Yohannes was rarely in a situation where he was not either gaining line or giving it back. But this was one of those times. He balanced high in the air in his harness, and waited for what seemed like a very long time before letting his impatience show. I could tell he needed something to pull against. I came down from the tower and steered from the bridge controls, thus giving Yohannes someone to glare at as he waited for the battle to change. Finally the tuna turned and Yohannes went to work pumping and winding. After giving back 300 yards of line, the tuna again dived, going straight down for more than 400 yards at a red hot speed. Yohannes now started to curse me and my "light" 130 pound tackle. Looking down from the bridge at the angler's mounting frustration, I knew better than to try to convince him that 130 pound test line was not considered light tackle.

The mood in the cockpit turned ugly as Yohannes's friends were complaining about the possibility of missing their afternoon Chalks seaplane flight and my two mates were sitting idly on the covering boards whispering to each other. Yohannes was not helping things either, since he was uttering strange words in Ethiopian, punctuated periodically with my name. But soon things began to change. Yohannes was gaining line and everyone was happy. Scottie leaped off the covering board and put on the tuna gloves. These gloves consisted of a thin leather inner lining with a wet outside cotton glove that had the last part of the fingers removed.

As Copper steered the chair, Yohannes started to crank as fast as I had ever seen. Making huge pinwheels, the bluefin could be seen deep in the clear water reflecting the afternoon sun. This silver flash was a good sign. It meant we had a tired tuna coming up. I called down to Copper and he in turn waved his pliers, thus acknowledging that he knew the tuna was to be released.

It took Yohannes an additional hour to get the fish to the boat. Once the wire was up, Scott took a wrap and started to pull. The tuna then pinwheeled down, and as he started to turn upward, I backed the boat inside the tuna's circle so that its head popped out of the water at the starboard corner of the transom. Scottie then took a double wrap, moved forward and pinned the tuna to the side of the boat. Copper immediately cut the wire that ran from the rod tip to the back of Scottie's gloves, thus leaving him holding only the last four feet of wire that ran to the hook in the side of the tuna's mouth. He then rushed to the transom corner to see the actual size of the tuna and watch it swim away once Scottie let go of the wire. Trying to get my camera out of the bench seat, I didn't understand why they were calling for me. I again told Scottie to let go of the wire, but Copper shook his head no and frantically motioned for me to come down to the cockpit. Fearing the tuna might die from exhaustion, I rushed down the side of the bridge and across the covering board. I placed one hand on Copper's shoulder to steady myself as I stood on the transom looking down at the tuna. Copper then told me that he was sure this tuna was much larger than the 842 pound bluefin we caught last year. As I ran to the bridge to get my camera, I told Scottie to let the wire go, but it was too late. Yohannes, overhearing what Copper had said, spun him around and pushed the straight gaff against his chest shouting, "Gaff!" Copperhead's reaction was instantaneous, the exhausted tuna was on one end of the gaff and both Copper and Yohannes were on the other end.

Once I put the meat hook in the tuna's mouth, we walked it to the corner and prepared to drag it through the door. We went through the same routine as always. We pulled on the tuna, and for the first time ever, it stopped partway through the door. I had pulled tunas over 800 pounds through this door before and never had a problem. Again we pulled and again we failed. This time we were joined by Yohannes and, after the old heave-ho, the tuna was still on the ocean side of the door. We were now joined by the rest of the group and, after the third pull, the tuna was now wedged tightly in the door. Luckily we had put a tail rope on its tail which allowed me to work it back and forth while everyone pulled on the rope going to the meat hook. Finally the tuna came in like a giant bar of soap and slid across the wet teak deck. I now started to think that Copperhead could be right about the size of this fish.

We were almost to Bimini before I looked down at the cockpit to compare the two fish. The last bluefin was definitely larger than the first. I then felt that my guess of 700 pounds for the first tuna was probably too high and never thought any more about the weight. We arrived at the Bimini Big Game Club and tied the boat to the dock next to the scales. Don Smith, the dock master, cheerful as always, strolled over to help weigh the two tuna. The first tuna was lifted out of the boat and then hung on the scales. A crowd gathered as Don called the weight down as 762 pounds. We all knew that the next one would be heavier. After lifting the second tuna out of the boat and up to the scales, Don was careful to weigh this tuna twice before calling out, "919 pounds!" This was the first giant bluefin tuna over 900 pounds to be caught in the Bahamas. It was also the heaviest game fish ever caught in the Bahamas at that time. The Commissioner soon arrived to verify the tuna's weight and, after he supervised the final weighing of the tuna, it still stood at 919 pounds. Yohannes's friends stayed over for the big party at the Red Lion where Yohannes had booked the entire back room for a dinner celebration. Most all the tuna crowd attended as did the Commissioner.

Yohannes Hekimian hugs his Bahamas Island record 919 pound blue fin tuna on the dock at the Bimini Big Game Club. The date was May 21, 1976. Standing at right is Captain Bill Harrison with mate Scott Taylor.

Captain Billy Harrison and mate man the tuna tower on board *Miltown III* on their way out of Bimini Harbour in search of giant blue fins.

Tuna Alley off Cat Cay in the Bahamas Islands. A typical school of giant
blue fin tuna migrating north to its feeding grounds off the coast of
New England. This aerial photo is courtesy of the IGFA from the
Dade Thorton Collection.

George Poveromo

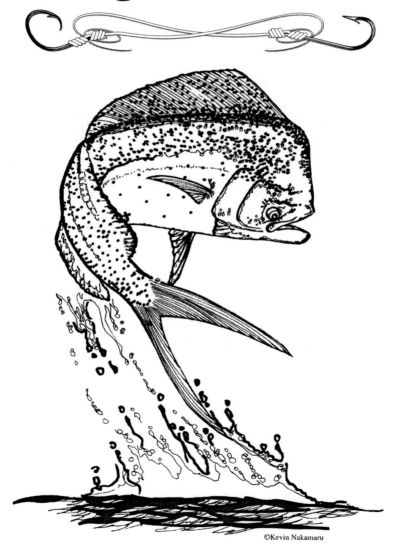

©Kevin Nakamaru

GEORGE POVEROMO

George Poveromo is a renowned angling authority who serves as a Senior Editor for Salt Water Sportsman Magazine, the nation's oldest and largest publication on the sport of marine fishing. He is also Executive Producer and Host of the ESPN2 television series - *George Poveromo's World of Saltwater Fishing.*

George's in-depth knowledge of marine angling is the result of a lifelong passion for fishing. In 1983 he was recognized by Motor Boating and Sailing as one of the top eight anglers in the country - at age twenty-three! He had fished along the entire U.S. coast, as well as Alaska, Hawaii, Bermuda, Grand Canary Island, the Caribbean and a number of Central and South American destinations. His numerous feature articles in Salt Water Sportsman reflect his extensive background and expertise in salt water fishing, and his *Tactics and Tackle* column ranks among readers as the number one department in the magazine. All of this has made George a household name among Salt Water Sportsman readers of the fishing and marine industries.

George is also well known as the producer and host of the immensely popular Salt Water Sportsman National Seminar Series, the nation's largest and most successful educational course on recreational marine fishing techniques. The National Seminar Series has been on the road for nearly two decades!

When he's not shooting for his TV series, on the Seminar Series tour, or traveling in pursuit of column and feature-story material, George can be found off South Florida or in the Bahamas fishing aboard his Mako twenty-eight foot center console - *MARC VI.*

MADNESS AT THE BUOY
by
GEORGE POVEROMO

Over the years, I've enjoyed hundreds of incredible fishing trips, many of them documented in the pages of Salt Water Sportsman and on my ESPN2 TV series, *George Poveromo's World of Saltwater Fishing*. It's funny, but the memories of all the good fishing adventures sort of blend together over time. It's the misadventures I just can't seem to forget about, no matter how hard I try. I'm not sure why, but I can recall every single moment of those outings gone bad as if they happened yesterday. You know the kind I'm talking about: the ones that cause you to sit back, reflect on what happened, and share a few laughs - if you were fortunate to survive! My friends and I refer to these trips as "character builders," and we've had some real winners.

One such trip occurred in June, 1992, when we decided to venture some 100 miles offshore, due east of Cape Canaveral, Florida. Our destination was a NOAA weather buoy anchored in 2,730 feet of water that transmitted information such as air and water temperatures, wind velocity and direction, and sea height to the NASA Space Center. Positioned beyond the Gulf Stream's eastern edge, the buoy served as a magnet for many species of game fish, which fed on the concentrations of baitfish that gathered around the floating structure and its mooring cable.

It was stories of yellowfin tuna at the buoy that had prompted me to plan the trip. I had talked friends Mark Bradfield, a Palm Beach personal-injury attorney, Jack Harari, an emergency-room physician in Boca Raton, and Casey Lynn, a technician with a major outboard manufacturer, into joining me aboard my Mako 261, *MARC VI.* In addition, friend Danny O'Neill would accompany us in his Mako 261, *Spin Off.* Danny's crew would consist of Chuck and Billy Gerlach, and Bill Munro of Ande Monofilament.

There was just one problem: our boats didn't have the fuel capacity to run 100 miles offshore, troll all day, and run 100 miles back. We solved that problem, in part, through the help of Barry O'Neill, Danny's father. Barry had talked his friend Al Levenson into taking his fifty-five foot Hatteras, the *Turtle,* along as a mothership. Barry would fish with Al aboard the Hatteras, with veteran South Florida captain, John Simes at the helm.

The plan was to load the Hatteras with several fifty-five gallon, Department of Transportation-approved drums full of gasoline to serve as the fuel supply for the Makos. We would run to the buoy early in the morning, fish all day, take on fuel, have dinner aboard the Hatteras, and spend the night offshore. We'd fish at night and be on the troll by first light, returning back to Port Canaveral Inlet by late afternoon.

After days of preparation and planning, the boats finally set forth from South Florida to our launch site in Port Canaveral. I trailered my 261, while Danny and Levenson traveled by water from Palm Beach. After docking at a local marina, we checked into our rooms at a Holiday Inn, showered up, and headed out for a bite to eat. I must admit that I didn't enjoy dinner very much. This wasn't due to any lack of quality food or lively conversation; rather, it had more to do with the stiff wind that had materialized.

Back at the hotel, I watched the weather report on TV. NOAA was calling for a 15-knot breeze from the west with seas raging from two to four feet and a sixty percent chance of thunderstorms.

Sure enough, the breeze was due west when we convened at the marina at 7:00 AM and discussed the situation. If we were making a local trip off South Florida, we would have called it off right there. A west wind in Florida usually means unsettled weather. Either a late-season front is on the way or there's a pressure system locked in place. Neither scenario is particularly encouraging when you're about to run over 100 miles offshore in two twenty-six foot center consoles. However, since so much planning and preparation had gone into this trip, I decided that we should at least venture out ten miles or so and see how things looked.

A west wind is misleading, at least on the eastern side of Florida. We cruised downsea in two to fours, enjoying a remarkably smooth ride. When we reached the ten mile checkpoint with no problem, we decided to proceed another ten and make our decision then. At twenty, we decided to push on to thirty, then forty. At fifty miles, we were committed. Onward to the buoy!

I felt excitement rekindling in me, and it was comforting to have Danny's Mako running alongside and Levenson's Hatteras not too far behind. There's something to be said about the peace of mind a large sportfisherman brings when you're far offshore in a small boat. It was a feeling that grew stronger as the trip progressed.

The seas were a steady four feet and peppered with weeds when we first caught a glimpse of the buoy. We were all fired up as we closed within a mile, slowed to trolling speed and dispatched a spread of plain and skirted ballyhoo. The weeds made it challenging to pick a route that didn't foul our baits, but we soon discovered a clear lane on the buoy's northern side. On the first pass we boated a forty pound yellowfin and a pair of dolphin, while the *Turtle* followed with a wahoo.

The quick action soon faded into an uneventful afternoon thanks to the west wind and lack of bait. Even the sargassum mats eventually disappeared. The seas flattened by 6:00 PM, allowing us to slip easily behind the Hatteras and refuel.

Just before dark, the eastern sky began to turn ominous, exhibiting the one thing you don't want to see 100 miles from land: lightning. Simes radioed us to say that his forty-eight mile radar showed a thick band of storms moving in from the east, and that bad weather was inevitable. He also volunteered to help knock down the seas by putting his bow into them and letting us tuck in behind him.

I vividly recall watching that solid black storm front making its way toward us and thinking how lucky we were to have taken on fuel. As the thunder grew louder, we laid down the outriggers, fishing rods and antennas, and donned our life jackets. It was going to be a wild ride aboard our twenty-six foot boats.

The storm front hit us with gusty winds and seas that went from calm to ten feet in about five minutes. With the bow of our Makos pointed into the seas some twenty feet behind the Hatteras, Danny and I held steady. Lightning was flashing all around us and the loud claps of thunder only kept us more on edge. A cold rain was driving hard into the cockpit, and it soon found a way through my foul-weather gear. Somehow I managed to zone out the elements and concentrate on using just enough throttle to keep the *MARC VI* pointed into the seas. Occasionally I'd catch a glimpse of Danny's boat either going airborne as he left the top of a wave or diving into the trough. My crew wasn't having fun, and no one said a word.

The front passed after forty-five minutes, leaving us with light rain, a steady breeze and a wind-whipped ocean. But we were okay. However, the *Turtle's* radar revealed more squalls moving toward us from offshore. We decided to play it safe, and embarked on a dark, seven hour run back to port. With any luck, we'd stay ahead of the next squall line.

With the Hatteras running behind us and keeping track of our position on the radar, Danny and I took off for home. The seas had dropped to a manageable six feet, yet it would still be a tough haul. Danny got the jump on me and settled into a comfortable groove. I tucked in behind him and used the seas he had knocked down to close within fifteen feet of his transom.

I've always been uncomfortable with following directly behind another boat, and this night was no exception. Call it a premonition, but I suddenly had the urge to break out from behind Danny's Mako and run alongside of him, which I did. Five minutes later, Danny's boat landed hard coming off a wave, causing Chuck Gerlach, who was standing behind the rocket launcher, to lose his balance. Gerlach ended up in the boat's splash well, hurting his ribs in the process. If it wasn't for the splash-well door and outboards, he would have gone overboard. And if that had happened while I was following right behind, he might have been killed. That's why I don't cruise behind other boats.

Once we made sure Chuck was okay, it was back to navigating the seas, guzzling Coca Cola to stay alert. The highlight of the run back was watching the GPS count down the miles to the inlet. Our enthusiasm picked up a notch every ten miles. When we hit the fifty mile mark, I told my crew that this was just like our typical run back to Miami from Bimini. At thirty miles I joked that this was just like our typical summer run offshore for dolphin. At twenty miles it felt as though we were just offshore, and when we hit ten miles to go, we felt close enough to swim to shore. Our trip was finally winding to a close, and not a minute too soon.

Battered and exhausted, we limped to the boat ramp and hauled my boat, then headed for the Holiday Inn for hot showers and some much-needed sleep. When we arrived, we were told that the hotel was sold out, save for one room. I took it and had two rollaway beds brought in. When I jumped in the shower, I discovered why the room was still available: there was no hot water! Too tired to argue with the front desk, I clenched my teeth, took a cold shower, and collapsed on the bed for four hours. By the time we checked out the next morning, the wind was blowing twenty-five knots.

A few months after our trip, the NOAA buoy broke its mooring and drifted into the Atlantic (it was later replaced with a smaller buoy). I wish I could say that I miss that buoy, but I'd be lying. Our terrible experience had filled me and every member of our group with a strong animosity toward the fabled Cape Canaveral buoy. But that still didn't make the trip any less memorable. Character-builders. You've got to love them!

DOLPHIN ON THE TROLL
by
GEORGE POVEROMO

There are numerous way to catch dolphin, but I love trolling for them. This passion can probably be traced back to my early adventures as a teen, when my friends and I lived for the excitement of watching dolphin come out of nowhere to attack our trolled baits. It's a thrill I never grew tired of.

Great memories aside, trolling is arguably the best way to score with these colorful, great-fighting fish, provided it's done correctly. Plus, there's always the chance of raising a marlin, sailfish, tuna or wahoo.

Over the years, I've tried to gear my trolling efforts toward bigger dolphin. While it's certainly exciting to get mobbed by school fish, I get a bigger charge over catching cows and bulls in the twenty, thirty and forty pound class. I'd much rather troll all day and land one thirty-five pound bull than catch twenty school fish.

To catch dolphin on the troll, early-morning departures are a must, at least in my book. I want to be working a weed line some 15 or so miles off the South Florida coast by 7:AM - not waiting in line at the local ramp. On a calm weekend day, you're going to face a lot of competition, which is why getting an early start and beating the other anglers to the weed lines and other floating objects is so important. By the time the other boats arrive on-scene, you'll have already tapped the area.

Long runs offshore are especially crucial in mid-summer, when the fish seem to be farther offshore. During June, July and August, I commonly run as far as thirty-five miles offshore looking for weed lines, weed patches, floating debris or pockets of flying fish. In summer, schools of bait, such as squid and flying fish, remain close to the surface during the cooler evening hours, which means that the dolphin will be there too.

When the sun rises and begins to heat the ocean surface, the bait moves deeper in the water column. This typically occurs around mid-morning. With nothing to keep them near the surface, dolphin follow their forage into the depths. If you haven't scored your fish before 10:00 AM, the odds of doing so afterward sink as rapidly as a thirty-two ounce trolling sinker. Most of your action will occur between sunrise and 9:00 AM, so plan your runs accordingly. The other beauty of fishing the early shift is that you're usually back at the ramp with your catch by 1:00 PM, safely ahead of those nasty afternoon thunderstorms.

I begin my preparations for a dolphin trip the day or evening before. I'll rig and brine my baits, rig my trolling tackle, and tie an assortment of jigs and hooks to spinning tackle for schooling fish. I'll load the boat with ice and have everything ready to go for the morning.

As soon as I clear the inlet, I go into 'search mode," scanning the water for signs that can lead me to fish. I'll watch for birds, weeds and debris, notable surface temperature changes, concentrations of bait on the surface and fishfinder, and any unusual ripples on the surface that may indicate the presence of cruising dolphin. Rigging baits and preparing tackle on the way offshore will greatly cut down your crew's ability to look for fish. When you clear the inlet, the priority is to hunt for fish.

As mentioned, weed lines are great places to find dolphin. However, simply locating one doesn't guarantee success. A main reason why dolphin frequent weed lines is to forage on the small fish and crustaceans that seek shelter in the tangle of vegetation. Therefore, take a few minutes to scan the weed line prior to dispatching your baits. If it looks devoid of life, continue heading seaward until a 'live' weed line is located. Find the bait and you'll likely find the dolphin.

The same applies to floating debris. Dolphin congregate around floating objects such as boards, logs and coolers to eat the baitfish that seek sanctuary there. The longer an object has been in the water, the more marine growth (e.g., algae, barnacles) it will accumulate. This attracts microorganisms, which attract small baitfish, which, in turn, attract dolphin. Therefore, if a floating object looks "new" and there are no baitfish present, don't invest too much time in fishing it.

Areas of scattered weeds are also good. Plenty of fishermen run seaward and become discouraged if they don't locate a textbook-perfect weed line. All too often they turn up their noses at tiny scattered weed patches. This could be a big mistake. Remember, dolphin are structure-oriented fish. In the open ocean, the tiniest clumps of weed can attract bait and game fish.

As I make my way offshore, I use my GPS to record the coordinates of any areas dotted with weed clumps and bait. If I don't uncover a major weed line, I can run back and fish these "secondary" areas. As a backup, if the ocean looks devoid of life, I will head back in to 600 feet of water and troll along the edge of the continental shelf. In some places the shelf edge features a gradually sloping bottom, while in others it drops abruptly into deep water.

Game fish, including dolphin, often patrol the edge during their migrations. When the Gulf Stream washes against the shelf, it often creates upwellings of nutrient-rich water that spark plankton blooms. These, in turn, attract bait and game fish. The "food-chain" effect is one reason the shelf is such a good area to troll, especially during the spring when the dolphin travel close to shore.

Diving birds can be as good a find as weed lines, as they often give away the presence of dolphin. Any diving birds, particularly frigates, should be immediately investigated. If the birds keep diving over the same spot as you approach, rest assured that they're over dolphin. If they keep moving away, preventing you from closing the gap, they're likely over skipjacks.

In the bait department, I almost exclusively troll large to horse ballyhoo. I'll rig some for swimming and some for skipping, and a few on wire with an Islander skirt. If I'm fishing exclusively for dolphin, I'll troll twenty pound-class gear, with a thirty pound-class outfit or two for the bigger baits. I troll with Penn International reels and matching Penn stand-up rods.

Since fluorocarbon became readily available to recreational anglers a number of years ago, I now use the material for my leaders. Compared to nylon monofilament of the same breaking strength, pure fluorocarbon is smaller in diameter, has very little stretch, and offers exceptional abrasion resistance. The latter is why I prefer it for trolling. However, the big selling point of fluorocarbon is that it's refractive index that is nearly identical to that of water. This makes it much more difficult for fish to see. In clear water, I've found it makes a big difference.

I rig my ballyhoo on ten feet of 130 pound fluorocarbon leader. I use an 8/0 long-shank, ring-eye hook on the large ballyhoo and a 9/0 hook on the horse ballyhoo. The bait with the Islander lure is rigged on ten feet of eighty pound stainless-steel wire. The swimming ballyhoo have a small egg sinker that rides tight to the bait's chin, while the skipping ballyhoo is weightless.

The swimming ballyhoo are generally fished from the outriggers and placed far enough back to keep them running just beneath the surface. I'll also stagger their placement by about fifteen feet or so. The outrigger baits track approximately 180 to 250 feet behind the boat. The center 'rigger has a naked skipping ballyhoo positioned some 100 to 200 yards back.

I also run a skipping ballyhoo from the short flat line and position it right where the prop wash begins to fade to clean water.

The long flat line bait - an all-blue or blue-and-white Islander/ballyhoo combo rigged with a wire leader and single 8/0 long-shank, needle-eye hook - is positioned forty to sixty feet behind the short flat-line bait. This bait is rigged with wire because it sometimes attracts wahoo.

Trolling speeds vary between five and seven knots. The key is to make sure the skipping baits are barely splashing on the surface, while the swimming baits are working just below. To keep the baits performing their best, vary the trolling speed and/or position of the baits as sea and wind conditions change.

As mentioned, I like to hunt for big dolphin. By using large and horse ballyhoo, my baits won't get attacked by small dolphin and have to be replaced. School dolphin may charge up to a big bait, but they'll have a difficult time eating it, which keeps it in play in for a bigger fish. Conversely, if you want to catch smaller dolphin, troll smaller ballyhoo.

When I want to have fun with school fish, I bring in the trolling gear and break out the eight pound spin tackle rigged with small bucktail jigs. To keep a school of fish active longer, I have everyone onboard begin by using the same color jigs. Once the school grows leery of that color, we switch to a different one, which usually fires up the school again. When the dolphin tire of jigs, we switch to plain hooks and pieces of ballyhoo. And when they grow leery of the ballyhoo tidbits, we switch to live baits, such as pilchards and even shrimp. Live baits will push just about any dolphin over the edge, no matter how hard they've been hammered.

Trolling for dolphin is an exciting challenge, and once you know a few tricks you can expect to catch them consistently throughout the season. The fun level is only heightened by targeting trophy fish, and it's the anticipation of catching a big bull or two that keeps me heading offshore year after year.

Wind whipped seas, gale force winds and lightning strikes all around, these two twenty-six foot open Makos, *Marc VI* and *Spin Off* struggle 100 miles offshore to make their way back to safety.

CPSIA information can be obtained at www.ICGtesting.com
Printed in the USA
LVOW10*0042111213

364743LV00001B/1/A